Praise for *Baptized in Tear Gas: From White Moderate*

"Elle Dowd is the only white writer I have ever encountered in this weird space of progressive Christianity talking to her cousins about their sin of racism who isn't making a dime from her book—100 percent of every dime she makes off this book goes back to the community she learned from. That's the best—far from the only—reason to listen to her or buy this book."

—Lenny Duncan, author of *United States of Grace* and *Dear Church*

"*Baptized in Tear Gas* is a powerful and honest reflection rooted in equipping others with the skills and tools to engage in transformative change. It's a necessary read, especially for white people in this time. With the protests in Ferguson and the movement they birthed as a core experience, *Baptized in Tear Gas* helps to expand our collective understanding of how people take action to change their communities and society."

—DeRay Mckesson, civil rights activist and co-founder of Campaign Zero

"As a former Evangelical Christian, I'm well versed in our religion's collective resistance to 'woke culture.' Wokeness is demonized as a secular movement, established to diminish the importance of Jesus. However, in Elle Dowd's transformative memoir, we see that the grueling fight to uproot white supremacy—christened and propagated by no less than our own church fathers—is indeed holy work. Dowd shows us that it's Christ himself shouting through the voices of our bullied, imprisoned, and murdered Black brothers and sisters."

—Brenda Marie Davies, creator of God Is Grey and author of *On Her Knees: Memoir of a Prayerful Jezebel*

"White people explaining abolition to other white people is part of the work. I'm thankful to have this book as a part of my arsenal that I can recommend to other white folks working through issues of police and prison abolition."

—Emily Joy Allison, author of *#ChurchToo: How Purity Culture Upholds Abuse and How to Find Healing*

"In *Baptized in Tear Gas*, Dowd's prose sears the reader's heart with the fire too few of us caught after the murder of Michael Brown. But in the ever-sharpening glare of white supremacy, Dowd casts a vision for a transformed people and church, showing by example how we can move past Dr. King's 'white moderate' into a faithful body willing to confront our own complicity and challenge the lies of American racism."

—Emmy Kegler, author of *All Who Are Weary* and *One Coin Found*

"Elle Dowd writes with a sober clarity about the demon of white supremacy in a way few white people have. She speaks to us not as any kind of white savior; rather, echoing John the Baptist, she emphatically points the way to a world where justice reigns and where lions give up their very nature to lie down with lambs. *Baptized in Tear Gas* is a primer for those of us who are white and seek a better world."

—Jason Chesnut, co-founder of The Slate Project and filmmaker with ANKOSfilms

"Through her own experiences of learning and unlearning during the Ferguson Uprising, Elle Dowd holds up a mirror for white people. She invites honest reflection on—and action in resistance to—the everyday ordinary ways whiteness, white supremacy, and specifically anti-Blackness show up in our thought, faith, and behavior. Digging beneath the same old surface-level narratives catering to white comfort, this book is thoughtful, real, faithful, and true."

—Rev. M Barclay, co-founder and executive director of enfleshed

"In 2014 I watched as the Ferguson Uprising unfolded on my phone screen through Elle's Facebook posts. Her ability to communicate what was happening, both through her posts and through this book, helped me shift from denial and fragility to action."

—Dani Bruflodt, creator of The Daily Page Planner

"While many books convict and educate white Christians about white supremacy, racial capitalism, and anti-Black racism, *Baptized in Tear Gas* compels and equips you to do something about these matters. With humility, honesty, power, and grace—and without an ounce of shaming—Elle Dowd will help you imagine your own journey from white moderate to abolitionist and will inspire you to get moving! You will be challenged. You will be changed. You will be grateful."

—The Rev. Mike Kinman, rector of
All Saints Church, Pasadena, California

"Elle Dowd is the real deal—passionate, thoughtful, and gritty. She is accountable to the communities she serves. This book is a much-needed addition to the antiracist conversation, one that moves white folks beyond basics to a passionate belief in abolition and liberation. It's a story that resonates because Elle's story is one that is shared by so many people. We can't wait to recommend this book to our entire community."

—Father Shannon TL Kearns and Brian G. Murphy,
co-founders of QueerTheology.com

"If you are a white person of faith wrestling with the state-sanctioned violence you witness in the streets of America, this book is a must-read. Dowd's stories and theological insights will steel our resolve for the next time we demand justice and are met with tear gas, white supremacist hatred, and our own insecurities."

—Nathan Roberts, pastor and community organizer in Minneapolis, editor of *The Salt Collective* magazine, and author of two books

"The opposite of protest tourism, *Baptized in Tear Gas* powerfully excavates the chamber of the human heart where joy, hope, and faith collide with fear, propelling a young minister out into the streets to learn anew what the gospel demands."

—Rev. Elizabeth M. Edman, author of *Queer Virtue: What LGBTQ People Know about Life and Love and How It Can Revitalize Christianity*

"While many white moderates arrive on corners of poor urban ghettos looking to do safe ministry among dark bodies in despair, I celebrate Rev. Elle Dowd's *Baptized in Tear Gas* for its daring audacity to confront the insidious white moderatism among folk who've been the ultimate provocateurs of oppression since 1619. Submerge yourself in the divine waters of these pages, repentant and reignited to enter (as Jesus did after his baptism) the wilderness of authentic, anti-capitalistic justice activism."

—Danielle J. Buhuro, author of *Spiritual Care in an Age of #BlackLivesMatter: Examining the Spiritual and Prophetic Needs of African Americans in a Violent America*

"If you're a white Christian and you find yourself on the sidelines quietly lamenting another story of racist violence, go read *Baptized in Tear Gas*. It'll get you off the bench. In telling the story of her own conversion, with all its sorrows and joys, Dowd reveals how each of us can move beyond milquetoast moderation and toward true, risky discipleship. There's an abolitionist inside you. Dowd will help you find them."

—Peter Jarrett-Schell, head pastor of Calvary Episcopal Church, Washington, DC

Baptized in TEAR Gas

Baptized in TEAR Gas

FROM WHITE MODERATE TO ABOLITIONIST

ELLE DOWD

FOREWORD BY
REVEREND TRACI D. BLACKMON

Broadleaf Books
Minneapolis

BAPTIZED IN TEAR GAS
From White Moderate to Abolitionist

Cover photo by Camille Couvez
Cover Design by Brad Norr

Print ISBN: 978-1-5064-7042-9
Ebook ISBN: 978-1-5064-7043-6

Mike Brown forever

CONTENTS

FOREWORD

I met Elle in the midst of a baptism.

Within the context of the Christian faith, water baptism is symbolic of rebirth. It is an acknowledgment of spiritual awakening that suggests—as a result of an encounter with the ministry of a radical, revolutionary rabbi named Jesus—something about you has changed and will never be the same again. Baptism in any medium is symbolic of awakening, and I would argue that in August of 2014, on the streets of Ferguson, Missouri, there was a baptism of the vilest kind that stirred the soul of a community and disturbed the sleep of a nation.

It was August 9, 2014, a warm Saturday afternoon, when eighteen-year-old Michael Brown Jr. was gunned down by a police officer in the streets of Canfield Green Apartments. Images of Michael's lifeless body lying in the street began to stream on social media as first residents of Canfield, then those who were nearby, and soon Michael's parents, and then young people from all over the city began to converge—holding vigil while his body remained in the streets for more than 4 hours. When Michael's body was finally removed, the people remained.

I saw Alice, Elle's daughter, first. I wondered who the parents of this bold and courageous black girl might be. This seven-year-old womanish child with dark chocolate skin and kinky hair who marched with her friend Kenna through the streets of Ferguson and beyond demanding justice for Michael Brown Jr. This womanish child wielded the megaphone and led masses in chanting the words of Assata Shakur: *"It is our duty to fight for our freedom. It is our duty to win. We must love and support each other. We have nothing to lose but our chains."* Elle chanted along.

As I read the words on these pages, memories came flooding back, and I realized time after time as this white woman showed up in the streets of Ferguson, often bringing Alice with her, she was not only standing in solidarity to resist the state-sanctioned violence wielded against Black people demanding justice, but she was also being reborn.

This book is a road map to liberation for white people. Elle offers a glimpse of transformation and its learnings along the way, a glimpse of the revelation that comes when one knows all liberation is intricately connected and grace sets us all free. A year later, Elle and Adam brought Alice to hear me speak at Christ Church Cathedral. During the question-and-answer session, Alice raised her hand and asked me: *"What do you love most about being Black?"* I answered and then asked her the same question. Alice replied: *"I love that I am beautiful and brilliant, and I can be whatever I want to be."* Yes, you can, Alice. You, and your mom, have nothing to lose but your chains.

—Reverend Traci D. Blackmon

AUTHOR'S NOTE

This book is not written on a chronological timeline but is instead gathered around concepts, lessons, and themes. It is a collection of my memories. On every page, I have strived to tell the truth.

PREFACE

I have almost reached the regrettable conclusion that the Negro's great stumbling block in his stride toward freedom is not the White Citizen's Counciler or the Ku Klux Klanner, but the white moderate.
—Dr. Martin Luther King Jr., "Letter from a Birmingham Jail"

This is a conversion story.

A story of baptism into new life.

This is the story of how God transformed a white girl from the suburbs of Des Moines, Iowa, to an Assata Shakur–reading, courthouse-occupying abolitionist with an arrest record who is hungry for the revolution.

This is not a book about how to be antiracist—not exactly. Although it does include some lessons I have learned.

I am not an expert in antiracism. I don't think any white person can be, but even if there are experts, I am not one of them. What I am is a mother of Black children with a visceral, vested interest in our collective liberation. I don't believe *antiracist* is a destination we can fully arrive at, a mystical place where we are perfectly free from our white supremacist indoctrination, but even if I did believe that, I am not there. I'm a person who has learned a lot, but I am still learning. All credit for any lessons I have learned should go to the Black women, femmes, nonbinary people, and MaGes (people of marginalized genders) who taught me. If you are looking for a book about how to be antiracist, there are many by Black authors and other people of color that you should read first. You should pick up works by Austin Channing Brown, Ijeoma Oluo, and Brittney Cooper. This is not a book on the history of our criminal justice system or the details of the abolitionist movement. You should read the works of Michelle Alexander, Angela Davis, Ruth Wilson Gilmore, and Mariame Kaba for that. I am not an expert in Black theology. For that, you should invest in books by James Cone, Katie Cannon, Kelly Brown Douglas, and Delores Williams.

Racism affects various groups of people of color in different ways. While this book at times talks about white supremacy and racism more broadly, it mostly focuses on the phenomenon of anti-Blackness in particular because of the way it relates to my family and story.

This is not a complete and total account of the Ferguson Uprising in Missouri. No book could do that. This is not even a complete and total account of my own small story within the Uprising. There are some things that can't be put into words.

This book is me making sense of my story within a wider movement.

I hope you can tell that I feel tension about even writing this book. Antiracism is full of messy choices. I went back and forth about whether or not it was the right thing to do. This is *my* story, which means it centers me—a white woman—in a historic uprising for Black liberation. I don't want to cast myself as a hero or a victim. I want to invite my white siblings into the risky work of the rededication of our lives and souls. I want us all to join together in dismantling white supremacy for the sake of the gospel and for our collective liberation. I know that white people tend to listen better to other white people. And, at the same time, white people take up too much space in antiracist movements. When I talked to Pastor Lenny Duncan, author of *Dear Church: A Love Letter from a Black Preacher to the Whitest Denomination in the US*, about this tension, he said to me, "Yes. Write as if that is true."

In some ways, this book is a memoir. In other ways, it is a theological reflection on an event, a flashpoint in our nation's history—the Ferguson Uprising. In other ways still, it is a love letter to my comrades, especially the courageous young Black activists. It is a confession to my siblings of color of my failings, and it is an exhortation to my fellow white siblings to avoid the pitfalls I encountered on my journey as we participate in the lifelong process of antiracist work.

Part of the way that white supremacy functions is to consider the individual experiences of white people as normative instead of heavily contextualized and to universalize our experiences. Our experiences are not universal, and in fact the individual culture of a place greatly impacts our worldviews. So as a way to own that and to invite your reflection on the ways your own backgrounds have shaped you too, I will share with you that I grew up in Urbandale, Iowa, an overwhelmingly white suburb of the capital city of Des Moines. It had the features common in a lot of white suburbs—strip malls, chain restaurants, good schools. I graduated high school with a class of about three hundred. It wasn't a small town exactly, but we all mostly knew or at least recognized each other. My dad grew up in Des Moines. My mom, whose father was an Italian immigrant who came to the United States after World War II and married my pharmacist grandma, grew up in Chicago. She came to the Des Moines area to go to college.

My siblings and I all went through the Urbandale public school system from kindergarten, with Mrs. Kilpatrick, all the way through high school. I was lucky. Urbandale is a good school, in many ways. But it was at least 90 percent white. Urbandale was so white that my Italian coloring made me vaguely ethnically ambiguous, comparatively, and

I bounced among the unofficial racially segregated tables in my middle school cafeteria. I had friends of color growing up, especially when I was younger. But as I progressed through high school and was encouraged to take as many advanced-placement classes as possible to get a head start on college, my friends of color—who were just as smart as I was—were pushed toward general classes to make sure they had grades good enough to play high school sports.

We learned about "racial issues" during Black History Month or around Martin Luther King Jr.'s birthday. Although there was always some tagline at the end of the lessons like "And the struggle is not over; the fight for equality continues today," we talked about slavery and Jim Crow as if they had nothing to do with our current reality.

Mostly we just didn't talk about race. I learned quickly that it was impolite to mention race at all. During one of my classes, I was asked a reading comprehension question that involved pointing out the character in a picture in a book. I said, "The Black boy." Another student said, "Wow. Racist. Why would you say that? He's clearly the boy in the red shirt." There were two boys pictured with red shirts, one Black and one white. But talking about race was against the unspoken social code. And in polite white company, saying "Black" was like saying a dirty word.

It's not as if I didn't say and think plenty of things that, looking back now, I know are very, very racist. It was just coded racism. In high school, when the predominantly Black Des Moines Public School basketball team beat our team, we called them "thugs" and made jokes about their low-sagging shorts. It wasn't even subtle racism. I know that now. These coded words are not at all subtle once you recognize their purpose. But I didn't realize it was racism because I didn't actually know what racism was. I grew up believing that unless you explicitly said the sentence "White people are better than Black people" out loud, you weren't a racist.

A major way that my racism showed up was in the ways I centered whiteness as the norm. One of my high school courses introduced me to womanist literature. When I read books by Alice Walker or Toni Morrison, I was opened to a completely different world. The novels I read changed me; they were a very early seed in my radicalization. But I said things like, "Wow, if being a normal woman is hard, imagine also being Black." Whiteness was the default in my world.

Reflecting back, I am embarrassed. If you would have asked me, I would have undoubtedly said that racism is wrong. I wanted to be a morally good person. But I had no sense that my liberation was wrapped up with the liberation of my siblings of color.

I was very involved with my Evangelical Lutheran Church in America (ELCA) congregation. I had felt a call to ministry since I was young. I spent my free time in elementary school making up Bible studies for my neighborhood friends. I don't remember my church ever speaking about race or naming white supremacy as a sin. If they did, it must not have been often enough or explicit enough to have made an impact on me. We didn't talk about sin as something systemic. The ideas I learned about sin growing up were mostly around "sexual immorality," like sex outside of marriage or being "homosexual." After the ELCA voted in 2009 to ordain LGBTQIA+ people and give churches the option to perform marriages regardless of sexual orientation, my home church left the ELCA and pushed me out when I pushed back. I wasn't out yet as bisexual, but just asking too many questions was enough.

I was in college at that time, majoring in religious studies, planning to go to seminary one day. My classes in the humanities taught me to keep asking questions. I traveled to Sierra Leone in West Africa as part of a peace and justice internship and met the children who would become my daughters, Alice and Jessica, who were two years old at the time. Alice would come to the United States at age six, Jessica at age ten.

I had gone on other mission trips, which have become almost a rite of passage for white youth and young adults. Going on these kinds of trips was another way to demonstrate that you were a good person. That you couldn't possibly be a racist. On my first trip to Sierra Leone, in particular, I brought with me a major "white savior" complex and very little understanding of the effects of slavery, colonialism, and neocolonialism. Over time, I started reading and learning more and noticing troubling patterns in the ways that many nongovernmental agencies (NGOs) and missionary-planted churches operated abroad.

I got married and lived in California with my spouse, Adam, who was a US Army officer at that time but now organizes as a Veteran for Peace. I spent the first four years of our marriage splitting my time between working in a church and religious school in California and traveling to Sierra Leone to be with my children.

My daughters are amazing. When I met Alice, she was small and sick but still chock-full of fierceness. As a toddler, she would stand outside the window of my hut and just yell *"Mommy Ellllllllle!"* at the top of her lungs until I let her in. She is an expert at letting the world know who she is and what she is all about. Alice would boss around the other children at the orphanage, even those much older. When they played school, she was the teacher. As a teenager now, she is still that way: a visionary, a leader, a communicator. She wants to be an attorney or a politician. She is a trained community organizer and loves lobbying at our state capital for racial justice, environmental justice, and other issues important to her. She charms every state congressperson she meets, getting firm yesses on the record for bills that were considered merely aspirational. Her emotional and social intelligence is higher than almost anyone I know, and her political analysis is spot on.

Jessica is much different than her sister, gifted and exceptional in her own way. When Jessica wanted to be let into my hut in Sierra Leone as a toddler, she would just silently slip in. She would be there for twenty minutes, standing sweetly right beside you, before you realized it. Sometimes she would do this while Adam was taking a nap, and he would wake up to her big, expressive eyes just staring at him. Even though Jessica guards her words carefully, she communicates volumes through her facial expressions. She is thoughtful and creative. She loves music and art. She paints gorgeous city skylines with acrylic on canvas. Learning music comes naturally to her; it is a part of who she is. When she came to the United States, she flew through the piano lesson books we got her. Her captions on her Instagram posts are insightful. She loves cuddling up in brightly colored fuzzy sweaters because somehow she is always cold.

I love them. So much.

Becoming a mother changed my life. I think this is true for every parent. But the specifics of our family story, especially as transracial adoptive parents, shaped how I thought about race, colonialism, racism, police violence, and other issues of justice. It affects my theology, my relationships, where I choose to live, the work I choose to do, and more. I have had to grapple with the complex ethics of adoption—especially transracial adoption.

I am intentionally keeping many of those details private out of respect for my daughters. Those stories belong to them, and they can choose to share them when and how they wish. But I will say that parenting these babies that I love so much is a major part of my identity and one of the primary motivating factors for me in my antiracist work. For those of you who are also parents or who have little ones in your life that you love, I imagine that loving these children has changed your identity and theology too. I imagine that your hopes, dreams, and worries for the children you love might also affect your own hopes, dreams, and worries. As you look at these children, perhaps you also have moments where you understand the heart of God a little bit better and God's own hopes, dreams, and worries for all children, especially the most vulnerable.

When I began the adoption process, I joined Facebook groups run by adult transracial adoptees who spoke up about what it was like to have white parents like me and Adam. Sometimes I felt defensive about the things the adoptees would say about white parents, but I stayed. I read the books they recommended. I relearned US history. I learned how to take care of my daughters' skin and hair. I wanted to be the best mom I could be for my children. These conversations and the resources I was seeking out made me more aware of the ongoing and systemic racism in our country, but it sometimes still felt like knowledge that lived in my brain, not something that was embodied in my heart or my gut.

Then Trayvon Martin was killed by neighborhood watch vigilante George Zimmerman in Sanford, Florida, in 2012. I heard about the protests in response. For the first time, I started to feel afraid for my babies and the racism they would experience in this country. I was shocked and angry. And this time, I was angry not just because what Zimmerman did was morally wrong. This anger was different. I was angry because I started picturing this happening to *my* loved ones.

We adopted Alice and brought her to the United States just as the Army moved us to Missouri. A year later, Black unarmed teenager Michael Brown was killed by white police officer Darren Wilson in Ferguson, and in the coming months, everything changed.

One thing that changed was me. I became an abolitionist.

Because racism affects every aspect of our society, there are so many angles of the antiracist movements to connect with. I was drawn to the abolition movement. Before the Ferguson Uprising, I had never even heard of abolition. I didn't know who Dr. Angela Davis is. I was taught that the Black Panthers were "violent," that (the docile, whitewashed version of) Dr. Martin Luther King Jr. was the model exemplar of protest. Although I had slowly begun to reject some of these narratives about Black power and resistance, I considered myself a pacifist and defined that concept very narrowly. I was uncomfortable with a lot of the strategies and tactics of radical liberation movements. It was the relationships I formed in Ferguson that challenged those views and opened me up to the world that is possible, a world without policing or prisons.

But while abolition focuses on dismantling our racist criminal justice system, it is even broader than that. As Ruth Wilson Gilmore, one of the architects of the abolition movement, has explained, *abolition is about presence, not absence.*[1] Abolition *is* about an end to prisons and policing, but it is also inherently concerned with what is next. In Chicago, where I live now, the city spends 40 percent of its budget on policing: five million dollars per day. That is money that could be spent on other programs: it could be used to build something new, something that gets at the root of crime to prevent it before it happens, and to create structures of justice and public safety that actually work.

Prisons and policing do not do the things that we say they do. They do not serve as a deterrent; in fact, they lead to more and more crime. Data show that when people have the things they need, crime and violence decrease. But white supremacy in our government, housing systems, and city development has intentionally divested from Black and Brown neighborhoods. Instead of giving communities the care they need to get at the root problem, our current system uses violent repression to keep Black and Brown people from stepping out of line.

Abolitionists are quick to explain that abolishing the police and prisons doesn't mean abolishing help. Instead, abolition is about building a system of community safety and care that protects everyone, not just the interests of white property owners or the ruling class. But abolition is not just about tearing down old systems steeped in white supremacy and those that serve racialized capitalism. Abolition is not a onetime event; it is an ongoing revolution, a rebirth, a continual renewal. It is a way of life. It is about redelegating our budget and our energy. It's about creating something different.

In the past six years, I have seen conversations about abolition become more and more common. In 2014, I hadn't heard of abolition. In 2016, when I talked about it to my seminary classmates, I was thought of as militant, radical, and unrealistic. During the uprisings in 2020, the Movement for Black Lives and activists in Minneapolis brought the topic of abolition to the mainstream. Now I see my seminary classmates explaining to others why defunding the police as a step on the road toward abolition is the necessary and moral choice. These days I organize as a leader with an abolitionist organization, Southsiders Organized for Unity and Liberation (SOUL), in Chicago and partner with other coalitions of Black liberation organizations to chip away at mass incarceration and to resist police violence through political education and teach-ins, community care and mutual aid, direct action, lobbying and electoral work, and every other tool at our disposal.

The conversation, the demands, and the tangible changes we have seen in the past few years are remarkable. There are still plenty of moments of posturing, empty gestures, and lip service. But at the same time, Dr. Davis, a former Black Panther and another one of the architects of the abolition movement, has said that "this moment holds possibilities for change we have never before experienced."[2] God is breaking through, and the Spirit is at work, urging us all toward our collective liberation. This is a kairos moment. I believe we could see abolition in our lifetime.

You can be a part of that. You can be an abolitionist.

Although I hope many different kinds of people get something out of this book, I am writing primarily to people like me. Well-meaning, well-intentioned white people. People from the suburbs. People from the Midwest. People who fill up the mainline protestant church where I am a leader, the ELCA—the whitest denomination in the United States. I hope that maybe you will see yourselves in parts of this story. This ongoing transformation has meant a lot to me. I want that for you too. Even more importantly, I want you to join me on this journey because people of color matter to God and because God's saving work is for all of creation. As a way of offering support throughout our own process of transformation, each chapter offers questions for reflection and discussion. As a way of challenging ourselves to move away from theoretical thought experiments and into concrete action—to gut knowledge, not just head knowledge—each chapter also offers suggested action items.

I assure you that any wisdom you might find in these pages is not original to me but was imparted to me through Black theologians, scholars, and activists. Racialized capitalism functions by exploiting marginalized people for the benefit of people with privilege. It is wrong for white people to profit off Black suffering and death, and I follow a Jesus who I understand to be anticapitalist, so I am donating any money I receive from writing this book to Black liberation organizations, Black activists, Black political prisoners, and Black families who have suffered a loss because of police violence. I started by donating my first advance to organizations founded by each of Mike Brown's parents.[3] I am donating my second advance to Black liberation organizations and activists, including one of the political prisoners from Ferguson who is currently locked up. I encourage you to also donate to funds for families and survivors of police violence and the Black freedom fighters in your own community.

I hope reading this book can help those of us who are white to be honest about our indoctrination into the lies of white supremacy, particularly around the racist criminal justice system, and be willing to examine them. I hope those of us who are church members can be honest about the ways that the white church has failed by cozying up to the empire, staying silent in the face of oppression, refusing to take action, and decontextualizing and depoliticizing the gospel in a way that diminishes its power in the world.

And I hope this honesty makes space for a transformation for all of us together into something powerful and beautiful and better than we could ever imagine.

1

PULLING BACK THE VEIL

Therefore each of you must put off falsehood and speak truthfully to
your neighbor, for we are all members of one body.

—Ephesians 4:25 NIV

My experience of the Ferguson Uprising didn't begin until
August 13.

The real story began earlier.

On August 9, 2014, unarmed teenager Michael Brown was
shot and killed by white police officer Darren Wilson. But
the story began before that too. I would later learn through a
report from the Department of Justice (DOJ) something that
Black people in Ferguson had known for decades: that racialized overpolicing of people of color had been going on in that
community for a long, long time. And the struggle for Black
liberation is older than the United States itself, beginning
perhaps with colonialism and the transatlantic slave trade.

But on Saturday, August 9, 2014, I wasn't in Missouri.

I was visiting family in Iowa. As Mike's body lay out in the street, baking in the hot sun for hours, I was surrounded by air-conditioning, comfort, and privilege. While I was taking videos on my smartphone of Adam doing a silly dance with Alice, people on Canfield Drive were pouring out their front doors, armed with their cell phones, tweeting about the gunshots they heard. While Mike's mother wailed and cried and begged to be near her son, I was at a princess-themed party with my seven-year-old daughter, Alice, who had moved to the United States only a year earlier from her native Sierra Leone. That day, I rubbed coconut oil on my daughter's dark skin and dressed her in a purple-and-white poofy dress and a tiara. I put a wish out into the universe that not only would she know that she is royalty, but the world would treat her that way too. At the same time, the dreams that Mike's parents had, their hopes for his future, bled out onto the asphalt. He had just graduated high school only days earlier, a hard-fought victory in a district that had lost its state accreditation.[1] His mom said he had been looking forward to starting college later that month.[2]

I didn't hear the news until late that day, after I had changed out of my princess party dress and into shorts and a T-shirt. I sat on the purple couch in my parents' living room and idly scrolled through Twitter to decompress when I saw a photo mash-up of an old black-and-white picture of white police with menacing dogs from what looked like the civil rights era alongside a modern color photo of police with growling dogs. The tweet said something like "Happening NOW in Ferguson."

I was familiar with Ferguson. In fact, I had just preached near there the Sunday before in a church in a neighboring city, Florissant, as part of my work for the Episcopal bishop's office. Not long before that, I held a meeting in St. Stephen's Episcopal Church in Ferguson and had eaten lunch at the Ferguson Brewing Co. nearby. I remember calling Adam afterward and saying, "What a sweet little town," and wondering if it might be a good place for our transracial family to live. I knew that it was important for my Black daughter to live in a place with racial mirrors, and Ferguson seemed so diverse. And charming and cute and . . . quiet.

So when I saw that tweet, "Happening NOW in Ferguson," I thought it couldn't possibly be Ferguson, Missouri. But as I kept scrolling through Twitter, searching on Google, and clicking on hashtags on Instagram, it became clear that it *was* Ferguson, Missouri. I saw a photo of a Black man in a tank top holding a sign written on cardboard that read, "Ferguson Police Just Executed My Unarmed Son."

What happened? I thought as I kept scrolling frantically.

At that time, I knew that police violence was real but figured that it was generally the work of a few biased individuals. I was in high school in an overwhelmingly white suburb in Iowa when Sean Bell was killed in Queens, New York. We discussed his death in my (all-white) AP US history class as part of a regular discourse on current events. I was horrified that Sean had been killed the morning before his wedding, that the cops had shot over fifty bullets into his car. The son of a law enforcement officer in my class lectured me about what a hard job police have, noted that Bell had been drinking, and hypothesized that the police viewed Sean's vehicle as a weapon and "feared for their lives." The loud majority of the class agreed that we should respect the police, not critique their split-second decisions.

So when Mike was killed, I kept looking for some statement from the police, a side of the story that would make sense of this situation for me. Looking back now, I can see how much of this was my privilege. I had been taught growing up that the police were our friends; they were who we should call when we needed help. Police often parrot the same script my classmate did anytime there is an "officer-involved shooting," giving the same justification—that the officer feared for his life—and questioning the character of the victim.

When Mike was killed, there were so many rumors. Police (and others) immediately began spreading gossip about what Mike must have been up to earlier that day—rumors intended to sully his character—but they were far more reluctant to release any details about what happened in the moments leading up to his death. Part of me wanted there to be some good reason that he was killed, even as another part of me was ashamed that I would ever even think something like that. But if Mike did something wrong, did something to deserve death, then maybe all it would take to keep my own Black child safe would be to make sure she never messed up.

Still, I couldn't make it make sense. How could a kid—*an unarmed kid*—do anything that would justify being shot down in the street? I turned to Adam and said, "There's nowhere for us to go, nowhere we can live to keep her safe."

For the next few hours, I was glued to my phone, watching people live-tweet a vigil where the Ferguson police showed up with dogs. Waves of confusion, anger, and disbelief came over me. I tucked my daughter into bed at my parents' house that night, wondering what kind of world she would grow up in. I felt determined to do something.

The stories and rumors and misinformation kept flying, in large part because the police refused to release information to the media. So I figured, maybe I would go see Ferguson for myself. It was only twenty minutes or so from my office in Downtown St. Louis. The news kept showing a town in flames, but that image seemed so incongruent with the sweet, charming town that I had visited so recently.

Over the next couple of days in Ferguson, various barricades were erected, stores were closed, and people were unsure about leaving their homes due to the unrest and disproportionately violent police response. The Episcopal church in Ferguson had a food pantry, and people were helping deliver food to those who were stuck inside. I decided that when I went into the office on Wednesday, I would bring donations with me to deliver to the food pantry in Ferguson.

In hindsight, it's clear to me that I was so desperate to *do something* because I couldn't bear sitting in the discomfort of my conflicting emotions. I felt guilt, the general, heavy white guilt in response to racism but also the specific guilt that I had brought my Black daughter from Sierra Leone to live in the United States, and now maybe I was realizing that the United States was not the beacon of hope and opportunity I thought it would be for her. All my internalized narratives and presumptions and beliefs were bumping up against one another, and it was profoundly uncomfortable. I was experiencing what is called *cognitive dissonance*: How could police be mostly good and yet instances of their brutality continue to repeat over and over? How could an unarmed kid be deserving of death?

When I walked into the cathedral Wednesday morning before our regular weekly staff meeting, it took me at least twice as long as usual because I kept stopping or being stopped by each person I came across. Stranger or not, we would look at each other and ask, "How are you doing? Are you OK?" I can't even communicate the kind of regional,

communal trauma this was. It was the only thing that anyone could talk about in those first few weeks. In the parking
lot, in the elevator, in the staff meeting, everyone I came
across had features of shock and exhaustion written across
their faces. I wasn't the only one refreshing the news over
and over for hours each night.

After our staff meeting ended and I had finished up some
work in the office, I headed over to St. Stephen's in Ferguson to bring the donations for the food pantry. I ran into the
priest there, and I asked, "What can I do for you?" He asked
if I would hold a youth event in Ferguson in a few months,
to show people that Ferguson was more than this one event
that had made it infamous. There was this feeling shared
by white people that we needed to make sure that everyone
knew that we weren't racist, that this wasn't "who we are."

I dropped off some things at the food pantry but kept
the bottled water in the back of the trunk of my red Nissan
Cube. I had planned to donate it too, but it was just so hot
and muggy in the August heat that something (maybe the
Holy Spirit, maybe pure curiosity) told me to keep the bottles of water and bring them to the protesters.

I knew that the protests were happening over on West
Florissant, near Canfield. But it was hard to get there.
Streets were blocked off by concrete barricades. I used my
GPS and got as close as I could, parking in the lot of a BBQ
joint on the corner.

As I stepped out of my car, I felt ridiculous and out of
place. I didn't know anyone. And I had come straight from
the office, so I was wearing a pencil skirt, a blouse, and high
heels. Everyone else was in jeans and tank tops or was shirt-
less. Many of them were wearing bandanas or had locks or
braids. Someone looked at me quizzically and asked, "Who
are you? Are you a reporter or something?" I wasn't quite

sure what I was, so I said, "Um, no. I'm . . . here to help," and offered a water bottle.

I didn't know how to describe what I was doing there. Was this really my fight? What was my place here? What kind of commitment would that be? What would my boss and my family and friends think of me getting involved with something CNN kept calling "violent"? So I didn't feel ready to call myself a protester. But I did feel pretty clear that it was hot as hell and people should have water.

What I saw shocked me. I had read every news piece I could find about what was going on in Ferguson over the past few days and watched plenty of livestreams, but somehow seeing it in person made it both more and less real.

There were dozens of police officers in dark blue and black, standing shoulder to shoulder across West Florissant, giant guns in their hands held diagonally across their bodies. Behind them was what I later learned is an armored urban tactical vehicle. People on the street called them tanks. There was a man on top peering through the crosshairs of a sniper rifle pointed at the people who were only several yards away. One hundred people or maybe less had gathered: Black, mostly young, angry, nonviolent. I could see that they were unarmed because almost all of the young men had taken their shirts off to deal with the sweltering August heat.

They raised their hands in the air as a leader chanted, "Hands up!" and the crowd responded, "Don't shoot!" a reference to the reports by witnesses that Mike had his hands raised in surrender when he was shot.

"This is an unlawful assembly," one police officer said over the loudspeaker. "Leave now. Go home."

"*Mike* can't go home!" one older woman yelled back, her voice on the edge of tears.

"We *are* home!" someone else yelled out. "*You* go home!" Despite being a majority Black suburb, the police force was almost completely all white. And this white police force in Ferguson did not live in Ferguson but instead lived in comfortable white suburbs twenty minutes away. People began chanting again.

The police, with no sense of irony and with armored vehicles clogging up the streets behind them, announced over the loudspeaker that the *demonstrators* were blocking traffic. Things were quiet for a minute, and then the police began advancing toward the crowd. A wall of dark blue, walking in menacing, synchronized steps. Yelling "*Move!*" in deep, booming voices as people scattered, screaming.

I had been passing out water bottles near the corner when they reached me. One officer waved his gun in my face. The officer next to him glanced at him, eyes flashing to the side, sending a message to his fellow officer with his gaze. Their faces were partially covered by gear, but his intention seemed clear to me. It was as if he was saying, "Chill out, dude. Look at her." That's when he called me "ma'am" and politely told me to get out of there.

I don't even remember getting into my car. I realized I was driving around, my hands and breath shaky. The barricades were still up throughout the neighborhood, so my GPS kept directing me to roads that were closed. I had trouble getting out of there and no idea where to go. I was crying and angry and stunned and afraid and driving in circles, which mirrored my dazed mind and swirling gut. I just kept making turns and turns and turns until I saw flowers, candles, teddy bears, balloons, and a long, deep-red bloodstain.

I pulled over near an apartment building in a place that I am not sure was a real parking spot, walked over to the memorial, and just stood there and stared.

How could this happen? I kept repeating to myself. *How could this happen?* I wondered that a lot over the next two years while choking on tear gas or jumping after a flash-bang or rinsing pepper spray from someone's eyes or running from the rubber bullets police shot at us. *How can they do this? How could this happen?*

The fact is, though, this has been happening for a long time.

Whether it was quick deaths in the streets or the slow death of denying resources to Black communities like medical care or quality education, I learned that Ferguson was not just an isolated incident. It was more than one bad police officer. The St. Louis Police Department proved this by continually electing racist, crooked cops as the heads of its unions. They made it clear again and again when, against the explicit orders of the Department of Justice, they wore bracelets that said, "We Are Darren Wilson," admitting to the public that Officer Wilson did not act in a vacuum. There was a saying in the streets: Ferguson is everywhere. And the story of St. Louis County is not that much different from stories in other places you may have lived: a history of economic policies like redlining and social patterns of white flight led to segregated communities, and white people carefully carved out around ninety different municipalities in St. Louis to stay away from people of color. But all of those municipalities required funding. Funding for mayors, city halls, police departments. And so because of pressure from the budget, police officers in places like Ferguson were told to ticket and fine their Black citizens, shaking them down and draining their pockets with steep financial punishments for petty offenses, enforced with intimidation or violence. These unjust practices are well documented in a DOJ report that was released after a thorough investigation of the

Ferguson PD in 2015. Policies like these have the effect of putting police officers in adversarial relationships with the community they are supposed to protect and serve.

This was not new to the Black residents of Ferguson.

It was more like the final straw.

But I had grown up flashing a smile at the young police officer who pulled me over or crying to get out of speeding tickets. The police were there to protect my interests in particular. As a white person who grew up in a white suburb and was raised by white parents, I never had the "talk" about how to deal with the police—a depressing rite of passage I would learn is common for Black people before they become teenagers. And so all of this seemed so bewildering to me.

When I asked "How can they do this?" the answer I heard from Black people was "Because they get away with it." When I asked "How can they get away with it?" the answer was "Because they always have." Ferguson was an anomaly in *my* personal experience of the police as a white woman, but it is everyday life for the Black and Brown people of this country.

The way I understood race growing up did not prepare me for these moments. I had learned in school about slavery and the civil rights movement, but those issues were always painted as something long ago and far away. The definitions of racism I had been given were shallow; they talked about particular biases and negative feelings about people of color that occasionally rose up in a few white individuals, a few "bad apples." None of the definitions I learned spoke to systemic injustice and disenfranchisement.

People who were "racist" were depicted as one-dimensional characters and considered "bad people," almost like supervillains. I wasn't taught about the ways that all white people are indoctrinated into white supremacy from birth, that racism was not just reserved for the "South," older generations, the undereducated, and lowlifes. I didn't understand that racism was something that every white person subconsciously learned and had to consciously choose to unlearn to even have a fighting chance of not replicating those same systems. The caricatures of "racists" as all bad and all evil made it harder to recognize that racialized biases are something internalized by all of us who are white—teachers, medical professionals, bankers, judges, pastors, and other people we typically think of as *good*.

With this thin definition of racism and hyperbolic distortion of *who* a racist is, it felt impossible to think of real people that I knew—or even myself—as racist. Racists were monsters. They were all bad all the time. They didn't coach little league or teach Sunday school. They didn't write thoughtful birthday cards or donate to charity. And so although I had begun to question and unlearn some of these narratives, it was hard to think of any person as being racist unless they fit neatly into the evil box I had been taught about. Any positive experience with a person seemed to somehow negate the possibility that they could be racist, as if being at all "good" would disqualify them.

The Ferguson Uprising was one experience after the next of having these neat boxes and definitions torn apart. It was jarring. The very framework from which I had been taught to understand the world became unraveled.

At times it felt like I had no idea what was true anymore. Sometimes it even felt like the end of the world. If you saw news clips and photos from that time, it felt downright apocalyptic. The air was full of smoke from tear gas and sound cannons and flash-bangs. People were running and screaming.

We were making homemade gas masks from instructions tweeted to us from Palestine.

It *was* the apocalypse. Not in the sexy, glamorized, romantic Hollywood version of the word. but in its truest meaning. The term *apocalypse*, or ἀποκάλυψις in Greek, is about revelation. It is about *pulling back the veil*. The apocalypse means knowing more clearly something that was true all along but was hidden for some reason.

In this case, for me, it was true all along that this country was founded on white supremacy. It was true all along that although I faced injustice as a woman and as a bisexual person, I had privilege beyond measure because of the color of my skin. It was true all along that the police in this country act to violently enforce the will of the state and that justice in this country is not even close to "color blind."

These things and more had been true all along. But I had been unable to recognize it. The truth was veiled by my own white privilege, my own internalized sense of supremacy, my own inept theology, my own worldview. It was veiled by the dominant narrative of race in this country, which says that racism is a problem that is over, that it was solved in the past.

Some truths I *did* know. Like in my AP US history class years ago, there was a part of me that *knew* that a groom should not be shot and killed on his wedding day, that *knew* that shooting fifty bullets into a vehicle was disproportionate, excessive force. That *knew* that those police officers were motivated by something besides fear. And on that day in Ferguson, there was a part of me that *knew* an eighteen-year-old should not be shot. But even the things that I knew deep within me were often overshadowed by the strength of the forcefulness of a dominant narrative that privileged whiteness overall.

There were the things, too, that I knew in my head but had not yet become heart knowledge. I had begun to learn more about the violent, racist history of our country. Motivated as a parent of a Black daughter,[3] I had been reading everything I could get my hands on about the Black experience in the United States, and it was clear to me that it differed greatly from my own experience.

But even the things that I knew and cared about academically still felt like abstract concepts to me. A veil had to be pulled back to move me from understanding on some level that racism was real to feeling it viscerally in my gut. It wasn't enough to learn theoretically about racism. Unveiling it meant having it feel real not only in my head but in my heart and body, understanding still only a fraction of the ways that Black people have *known* these truths on a much deeper level for a long time.

I know that my church growing up, like many white-majority mainline churches, did not equip me to resist the evil of white supremacy and all of its empty promises. It did not help me pull back the veil. Instead, my upbringing in the church focused on individual morality with very little talk about the importance of systemic justice. I can only guess that the leaders of the church believed the mantra of white moderates—that to talk about such things was considered being "political" and being "political" was to be avoided. After all, sex, money, and politics are the sorts of things you don't talk about in polite company.

Not only did the faith community of my childhood not engage issues like race or police brutality; the stories I heard of Scripture were often hyperspiritualized and depoliticized too.

And I am not alone. I remember retelling the story of Good Friday in recent years to a friend who had grown up in the church. She had faithfully attended worship her entire life, had read the story of Good Friday and Easter every single year. Yet when I talked about Jesus being arrested and beaten by the police, as named explicitly in the gospels, my friend said, "I had never thought about Jesus as a victim of police brutality. I never realized he was arrested." But it is right there in the text: "So Judas brought a detachment of soldiers together with police from the chief priests and the [religious authorities], and they came there with lanterns and torches and weapons. . . . So the soldiers, their officer, and the Jewish police arrested Jesus and bound him. . . . One of the police standing nearby struck Jesus on the face."[4]

It wasn't until I read Dr. James Cone's *The Cross and the Lynching Tree* during the Ferguson Uprising that it became clear to me, too, that Jesus was profiled and arrested. He was beaten by police. He was dragged from kangaroo court to kangaroo court, where they railroaded him with a sham of a trial until ultimately he was executed by the state. Even though this is something we can plainly read in the gospels, this story had been buried under theologies that erased the political realities of the time. Perhaps because acknowledging them felt dangerously close to our own current realities. This truth was concealed by the mainline church from me and from many others like me. It was hidden from me, and like the truths of my own complacency, the truths of the reality of race in our country, it had to be revealed by a massive and ongoing unveiling.

My faith as a Lutheran teaches a lot about hidden truths becoming revealed. We talk about how God often feels mystifying to us, that God can often feel hidden. We don't understand God. God is a mystery. And yet there are ways that we learn more about God, that God becomes revealed to us: through nature, through art and music, through our relationships. But Lutherans believe that the truest revelation of God is found on the cross, in Christ crucified.

Michael Brown is not Jesus. He was a teenager, a kid. He should be alive today, flirting with girls, having rap battles with his friends, taking care of his younger siblings. He should be graduating college or falling in love. He did not choose his martyrdom, and he should not have had to die for racism to become real to me or to anyone else. But his death did unveil a lot for many people in the United States. The truths about racism in our country that had been obscured or glossed over by convenient dominant narratives that serve to protect the status quo were now being made clearer as these false narratives were peeled back, layer by layer.

Pulling back the layers of our indoctrination into the death cult of white supremacy is hard and holy work. It is our job to unlearn the narratives that this racist society has taught us. It is our job to examine these narratives carefully, to look for patterns, to ask where these ideas are coming from and who benefits from them.

In Lutheranism, the belief that God is revealed in Christ crucified is known as the *theology of the cross*. The theology of the cross tells us that we can see and experience God most clearly not in moments of glory but in the eyes of our suffering neighbor. Who God is is most apparent in the lives and experiences of those *who are still crucified today*. We say that we want to know Jesus, but white Christians often refuse to see Jesus present all around us in people like Michael Brown, Tamir Rice, George Floyd, Rekia Boyd, and Breonna Taylor. Our perception of who Jesus really is has been obscured by the sin of white supremacy. Our awareness of the reality that Jesus entered into during his time on earth is concealed, by design, by the elite ruling class in this country that benefits from our ignorance.

We live in a country that continues to execute Black people when white people perceive them as stepping out of line. As Dr. James Cone taught us, crucifixion was a type of death by lynching, meant as a deterrent to anyone who challenged the empire and the status quo. It was a political tool of repression and violence against not only the person being crucified but others thinking about rising up or fighting back.

The violence of the state is propped up by conservative churches that glorify it and perhaps even more by white mainline churches who remain silent. Many white people in liberal, progressive, or even so-called woke spaces have trouble believing just how violent things are for people of color in this country. Even when we are face-to-face with their stories, view the data, and read the extensive reports, white people often find ways to diminish the seriousness and pervasiveness of racism. But the truth is out there; it is tenacious and refuses to be hidden. The reality of the horrors white supremacy has wrought may be hidden by those who benefit from denying their reality, but they cannot be hidden from God. The blood of the crucified cries out from the ground. The voices of the prophets ring out in the streets. Even before viral hashtags, Black people and other oppressed minorities in the United States have been crying out in pain and in power, demanding justice, demanding their human dignity be recognized. And God continues to reveal truths to white Americans and to everyone else in the stories of our siblings of color.

If we would only listen.

Until we decimate the white supremacy obscuring our view, we will never recognize Jesus in our neighbor, and we will never clearly know him. When we as white Christians read our sacred texts, we have to start acknowledging the way that this ancient story still echoes throughout our own time. So many things about language and culture have changed since Jesus's time on earth. Empires have risen and fallen. New empires have replaced them—new governments, new ruling classes, new economic systems. But despite all of the differences in these past two thousand years, some things are chillingly similar.

Like police and soldiers occupying land that doesn't belong to them, seizing control, regulating the movements of the people, curtailing their freedom, as the people yell back, "We *are* home. *You* go home!"

Like the ways that religious leaders often cozy up to corrupt states, making unholy bargains in exchange for our own power, protection, and relevance.

Like the ways that people in power pretend to have no power at all, saying there's nothing they can do, washing their hands of innocent blood.

Like the crowds that cry, "Crucify him!" to silence and erase rabble-rousers and freedom fighters—or the modern-day equivalent: "All lives matter!"

Mike Brown is not Jesus. But his death has more in common with Jesus's death than we are comfortable admitting. When we betray Mike Brown or Philando Castile or Laquan McDonald by excusing their deaths, we betray Jesus. When we deny the obvious white supremacy at play in their crucifixions, we deny Jesus. The white church needs to decide which side we are on. Are we on the side of Jesus and the crucified ones in our midst? Or will we continue to align with those who crucified him?

Reflection Questions

1. What narratives did you learn about race and racism?
2. What did you hear growing up about the police?
3. Where were you when you first heard about Michael Brown's death? What was your first reaction? What kind of internal narratives did you experience being played out in your personal reflection? What kinds of conversations did you notice about that murder (or others) among your family and friends? What narratives did you notice in the media? Was there a turning point for you? Which story was that? (Was it Trayvon Martin? Was it George Floyd?)
4. Elle shared that a sense of guilt as a white person and a parent led her to "do something," ultimately resulting in her joining the protests. If you are involved in activism, what or who led you there?
5. Elle makes a point to explain that the majority of Ferguson police officers do not live in Ferguson. How might living in the community they serve impact police officers' daily work?
6. On page 9, Elle writes, "Ferguson is everywhere." Racial violence is a part of our culture in the United States. How has white supremacy polluted your community?

Action Items

• Talk to your pastor about reclaiming Holy Week to center the crucified in our midst and tell the truth about state violence. Consider how this might show up in the way you do traditional Holy Week commemorations and spiritual practices like the Adoration of the Cross or Stations of the Cross. Prioritize Black voices and the voices of other people of color. Dr. James Cone's book *The Cross and the Lynching Tree*[5] is a good resource for this. *Luther's Small Catechism with African Descent Reflections*[6] might be another place to start.

- Discussions of the injustice that happened in Ferguson are everywhere. Research antiracist organizations in your community and commit intentional time to listening and learning from their stories and missions. Redistribute your resources to support their work.

2

RELEASING CONTROL

By the baptism of his death and resurrection, your Son Jesus has carried us to safety and freedom.

— ELW Leader's Guide, Holy Baptism II

I kept showing up to demonstrations in Ferguson. It wasn't hard to do in those early days, logistically. Something was happening almost 24/7 for the first several months— from bigger rallies and marches to strategically planned creative direct actions. Perhaps more striking than any of that, however, was the constant presence of people just there, outside, holding vigil. At any point during the day or night, at least a handful of people would be posted at the empty lot of the burned-down QuikTrip or, later on, across the street from the Ferguson Police Department.

That's how we first got to know each other, just hanging around with signs in the same place and introducing ourselves. Eventually, faces and names became familiar. And on the days and nights when things were really scary, we formed the deep bonds of people going through something truly terrifying together.

Each day, I would finish up at the office and check Twitter for an update. I learned to check the #MikeBrown and #Ferguson hashtags first to know what sort of situation I might be walking into because the police were so erratic and unpredictable. Then I would just go where the people were. Sometimes I brought water bottles to share or a folding chair, although for a period of time, the police threatened to arrest anyone who stood or sat still and didn't keep continually marching.[1] This didn't stop us; people walked for hours, and some creatively found loopholes and protested on bikes. This policy was later challenged in the courts—there is no "five-second rule" in the First Amendment, and requiring people to continually walk instead of standing still violated our constitutional rights to free speech and assembly—not to mention that this unconstitutional policy persecuted anyone with physical disabilities.

When I would head up to Ferguson, I tried to remember to bring more sensible shoes and would slip on some ballet flats, leaving my six-inch heels in the car. This became more essential on the nights I stayed after dark, when it was important to be able to run when the police started using tear gas or rubber bullets. But even on the days I forgot to bring my flats with me, I was still out there, standing in my favorite Jessica Simpson platform stilettos. I made sure to leave a handmade cardboard sign in my trunk that read "Black Lives Matter" so that I could make my intentions clear and wouldn't keep getting mistaken for a reporter.

I remember hearing early critiques that the protesters in Ferguson "didn't have a plan" or were somehow disorganized or "didn't know what they wanted." That couldn't have been further from the truth. I saw a list of demands almost immediately. And on Twitter, people made plans quickly. Less than a week after Mike Brown was killed, there were tables set up in the empty QuikTrip lot, and someone would be there to check people in and get people connected—people who brought water, people who brought food, people who brought supplies to treat tear-gas injuries and make homemade masks, legal observers, street medics, and those who created art and banners.

For the first time—or at least the clearest—I was seeing the "Body of Christ" in action. Direct action work in particular and Black freedom fighting more broadly have an extensive body of knowledge, theology, proven history, and established praxis. I was completely unfamiliar with this body of knowledge then. But I was still able to notice that something profound was happening in front of me. Just as 1 Corinthians 12 describes the people of God as an assembly full of many different members with different varieties and gifts who work together, like a body, to serve God and one another, I was seeing the activists in Ferguson work together for the cause of justice:

> To each one the manifestation of the Spirit is given for the common good. To one there is given through the Spirit a message of wisdom, to another a message of knowledge by means of the same Spirit, to another faith by the same Spirit, to another gifts of healing by that one Spirit, to another miraculous powers, to another prophecy, to another distinguishing between spirits, to another speaking in different kinds of tongues, and to still another the interpretation of tongues. All these are the work of one and the same Spirit, and [God] distributes them to each one, just as [God] determines.

Just as a body, though one, has many parts, but all its many parts form one body, so it is with Christ.[2]

There are all kinds of different gifts and abilities and roles to play in a movement. We need each other, we rely on each other. No body part or member or role is more important than another.

What I saw in Ferguson was that these people—many of them first-time activists, although not all of them—showed up and brought their whole selves. Toddlers hung on the backs of young mamas with megaphones who were leading chants with fierceness. The people who were communicators communicated; they livestreamed, they tweeted, they wrote and organized newsletters. The artists created; they made giant papier-mâché pieces, powerful posters, brilliant banners. People with health care backgrounds worked together with street medics trained during the Occupy movement. Law students ran legal clinics and assisted with jail support. Members of militant Black liberation groups directed traffic as people drove by in their cars and honked support, yelled out their windows, raised a fist in solidarity.

It was powerful. And moving. And confusing. It was really disorienting to see one thing with my own eyes and watch a totally different story play out on CNN later. One night, I remember seeing the police throw a tear-gas canister, which caught a bush on fire. The police's narrative was that *protesters* lit the bush on fire, but you could clearly see it was the canister there at the base of the shrub that had ignited it. Yet certain segments of the news media would parrot whatever the police said, doing none of their own investigating, reporting it as fact. And I was left trying to answer random acquaintances on Facebook, people who were never in Ferguson but were so sure they knew exactly what was happening, demanding to know why I kept defending people who were "so violent."

But I didn't see anyone violent—except for the police.

I saw people act in self-defense. I saw people who were deeply traumatized from generation upon generation of systemic abuse. I saw people fighting to love themselves, reclaiming their dignity, demanding to be heard. I saw people who were passionate, people who *wanted to live*.

I didn't see violence.

I wasn't always clear on this. Questions of violence are one of the primary ways that well-meaning white "allies" undermine the work of activists of color. We have to do more analysis about what actually constitutes violence and what doesn't; otherwise, we will simply remain part of a violent system that works against freedom for people of color.

I frequently felt apprehensive, especially early on in Ferguson, about anything that might be construed as "violent" by the white people I had grown up with. I had never before thought critically about how we define violence. I had no power analysis because no one in my white suburban upbringing had taught me to ask, *What counts as violence? And who gets to decide?*

When the police chief or the mayor or the governor would instruct protesters to be nonviolent, the protesters would rightly retort, *"Tell that to the police!"* The police were the ones who had killed an unarmed teenager and then let his body lie in the street for over four hours. The police were the ones who had shown up to a candlelit vigil with dogs and riot gear. The police were the ones in armored vehicles that looked like tanks who fired chemical weapons on crowds, kettling them—surrounding them so that they couldn't escape—as they coughed and choked on a substance that had been banned in warfare abroad by various international treaties.

So I agreed that the police, not the protesters, were the ones who needed to be told to be nonviolent. But I was still uneasy about things protesters were doing, like defying orders and standing in the street. I now know that there is nothing violent about standing in the street. What I felt was discomfort because I had been socialized to bow to authority, not to challenge it. I wanted to control the image of the protests, to protect it, because I really thought that if everyone just *behaved*, then maybe people would *listen*.

On the few nights where there was some property damage, like the burning down of the QuikTrip that first week of the Uprising or the breaking of windows on that November night the grand jury failed to indict Darren Wilson, I was so incredibly distressed. Growing up in a middle-class neighborhood in a capitalist society, I had been taught to put a high value on private property. We believed in the so-called American dream and told each other a lot of stories about the value of hard work. We ascribed worthiness to a person based on what they could produce. Your house, your job, your car were all reflections of hard work and, therefore, your character. The middle-class and upper-middle-class people in my community growing up worshipped property. They even wrapped it in religious language sometimes, humble-bragging about how "blessed" they were. I internalized shame about this, spending my early years growing up in a blue-collar home. My dad was a mechanic. I saw that he worked just as hard to provide for us, harder than people much wealthier than us. But I still believed this narrative of meritocracy somewhere deep inside of me, that people earned what they got and got what they deserved. Destroying people's property, then, was seen as an attack on them as people by taking away the things they had worked so hard for.

I believed smashing windows was violent, that it detracted from our cause and diluted our message. I know now that in many ways, it actually enacts the message. In a capitalist society, people with the least amount of power deciding what happens to capital, at least in the moment, is literally an idea becoming enfleshed. Besides, the fact is, if people are not moved by the very real pain of communities terrorized by state violence, broken windows or not, they will not be convinced. After Freddie Gray was killed in Baltimore that next April, I watched how little media traction there was until the CVS was destroyed. I realized that no one would've noticed or cared about Ferguson either if that QuikTrip hadn't burned down. I wondered if that was the real violence—ignoring the pain of people screaming for help, turning away from blood-soaked streets and broken spines, becoming scandalized not by a culture of death but by the destruction of property. Maybe that was real violence. And I had participated in it.

I've come to realize that property damage is contextual. There are some forms of property damage—like the burning of Black churches—that are violent. They call upon a history of oppression and terror. Other forms of property damage—like damage to corporate property, carried out by oppressed groups who have been silenced and ignored—are not violent at all. They are a *result* of violence. Like Dr. Martin Luther King Jr. said, "Summers of riots are caused by . . . winters of delay."[3] There are no funerals for broken windows because broken windows can be replaced. But the life of a loved one, a child, a human being cannot be given back. No insurance policy can resurrect someone killed by the police. There is no coming back from that.

It was frustrating to see how much coverage was given to a few isolated incidents of property damage in Ferguson, especially when property destruction didn't happen the vast majority of nights during the protests. I was exasperated by the shoddy reporting that seemed to insinuate that those "looting"—or what I now call "redistributing wealth"—and the protesters were the same people when they most often were not. I noticed how little media coverage the young Black folks who swept the streets and cleaned up each morning got, while the one image of a burning car was played by news stations on a loop, repeating for months as if all of Ferguson was constantly burning.

The Black activists and thinkers around me had challenged me on my definitions of violence. I realized how often white people consider literally anything Black people do to be violent. Pastor Traci Blackmon once told me, "Black people will never be unarmed as long as our Blackness is the weapon they fear." We saw this play out in Ferguson, where the officer who killed Michael Brown said that despite being unarmed, the teenager looked "demonic." No weapon was needed; Mike's skin was enough to be considered a threat.

I began to see the absurdity of calling the unarmed, chanting crowd that simply refused to leave the street *violent* while ignoring the clear and obvious show of force by the armed representatives of the state. I started to question, the voices of activists ringing in my ears and heart, why people cared more about broken windows than broken spines. I learned that state violence is so pervasive that it has become normalized. The state has declared a monopoly on violence, so we call breaking windows violent and somehow think that denying people adequate housing or education or health care is not.

I learned from people in Ferguson about counterintelligence programs in the 1960s and 1970s. I discovered how, historically, radical movements are often infiltrated by agent provocateurs, people paid by law enforcement to cause problems so that the state can justify their resulting, violent repression. On the night the grand jury announced their failure to indict Officer Darren Wilson for the murder of Michael Brown, I was outside the Ferguson Police Department with a large crowd. Once the announcement was made and people responded with chants, I saw the police getting into formation. I was across the street by a warming station because it was so freezing cold. Things were tense, emotions were high, and then . . . *pop, pop.* I saw a man in a hoodie fire a gun into the air twice and then run around to the back of the police station. And then the police advanced on the crowd. If I hadn't seen this for myself, I would've thought it was a wild conspiracy theory. But it happened, and it's still happening now.

So I think of violence differently now. I remember the rare cases of property destruction, and I see traumatized people who were the true victims of violence themselves, crying out to be heard. I see anger and defiance as valid responses—not inherently violent—especially when you are fighting for your life. I see "looting" or "the redistribution of wealth" as justified by people whose communities have been robbed of resources, whose very bodies were kidnapped and stolen, whose labor built this country, and who never saw the financial benefits or received reparations for its horrors. I see disruption and resistance as targeted self-defense in the face of an ongoing genocide.

This was not how I felt at first though. I held on tightly for a long time to my narrow, uncomplicated beliefs about peace and violence. I had convictions. I thought I knew better. I had all sorts of ideas about how things should be run in this movement.

There was a part of me that knew that what I was witnessing in Ferguson was historic and holy. This is the part of me that pulled Alice from her first day of first grade early and drove her to a march organized by the local clergy. There was a tug in my heart, a bit of wisdom from beyond me, that kept nudging me and saying, "This is important. You should be there." But there was another part of me, too, that was naive and green and had no idea what I was doing and had no framework to process what I was experiencing. I was completely lacking in self-awareness about how foolish I truly was.

On August 15, a little less than a week after Mike was killed, I was back at the empty QuikTrip lot where people were gathered. Although it seemed like everyone around me was organized and ready, I still wasn't totally clear what the hell I was doing there. I just knew I felt this strong pull to be present, so I continued to go every day since my first encounter with the riot police. I again brought water bottles to hand out. At this gathering, I was handed a flyer that read, "#FergusonOctober." I remember thinking to myself, *October? This will have blown over by then, surely.*

I had no idea.

Even though they had refused until later to release the name of the officer who killed Mike, even though the police kept defaming Mike's character with rumors that he was nothing more than a "thug" who deserved it, some part of me still believed people would do the right thing, that the system would work, that there would be some kind of justice. How could they ignore the faithfulness of all of these demonstrators? By this time, the Ferguson police had roughed up and arrested well-respected journalists from mainstream media outlets, bringing even more national attention to what was going on there. I thought that if people just knew what was happening, surely everything would work out.

So when a Black woman handed me that flier, I took it with a smile and then noted my critique to Adam—that by waiting so long to hold a national event, they were going to lose momentum. I thought that holding an event in October was ridiculous. That was two full months away. Looking back, it is embarrassing to think how certain I was about things I clearly knew nothing about. Even though I wanted to support the Uprising in Ferguson, the movement that was forming, I was constantly and silently critiquing everything around me.

A variety of demonstrations happened in St. Louis and Ferguson during these times. Led by different people, each demonstration used different strategies and different methods. In the beginning, I felt really comfortable with some of the big marches held during the day. These marches were typically multigenerational and multiracial. They often had a big contingency of clergy and were planned well in advance with a lot of communication about routes and expectations.

Other marches and direct actions made me a lot more nervous. In the early fall of 2014, I remember marching to an unknown location. At one point, the young people leading us turned us around and went another direction. I asked the person next to me where we were going, what the plan was. They didn't know. I didn't know. Who were the leaders here? Did the leaders even know? *Did anyone know?*

There were chants all around me. People on megaphones chanting one thing, people a little ways back chanting something else. I felt my chest get tight, first with anxiety and then with impatience. Why didn't whoever planned this make an actual plan? Why wasn't it communicated to me? Why didn't I know what was going on? At one point, I thought to myself, *If I was in charge, I would have made a map for everybody.*

If I was in charge.

Since then, I have learned that this feeling of frustration and impatience, this idea that I somehow knew better than the leaders of this action what to do in any given moment, was born out of my own internalized sense of racial superiority. I had grown up being told from the time that I was very young that I was a leader. I was praised by my family, my friends' parents, my teachers. I received leadership award after leadership award. I earned scholarships based on my "ability to lead." I looked around at the young Black people directing this march, and even if I wouldn't have said it this way, a part of me really thought I could do it better than they were.

The only grace here is that I kept my mouth shut at this moment instead of voicing my critique out loud or, even worse, trying to take over and take charge (although when some other white clergy members made this mistake, they were quickly and firmly corrected).

What I attributed at the time to incompetence was actually a complex set of factors that I had no experience dealing with. The reason many of the actions led by young Black (often queer) people weren't, in my mind, "clearly communicated" beforehand is that sharing that kind of information in a Facebook event tipped off the police, putting people's safety at risk. Plans seemed to change from moment to moment because these leaders needed to make split-second decisions about strategy and safety, knowing far better than I did how real the danger was.

And perhaps most importantly, the reason that I didn't know every detail of every plan was because *I had no business knowing*. I was so used to being at the center of things, so used to being praised as a leader, so used to having (white) people come to me in my own (white) community for advice or ideas that I assumed that even in the midst of another community, I was entitled to some sort of position of leadership or at least knowledge. I understood that there were so many reasons for Black people to distrust well-meaning white, liberal women. But I believed, on some level, that I was different. I was one of the good ones.

Angel Carter, one of the activists, would post this message from time to time on social media: "All critiques of the Movement must be delivered to the front lines, in person. Thanks, The Management."

This was a way of reminding Monday morning quarterbacks who didn't have to make snap decisions in the midst of clouds of tear gas that things were not as simple as it might seem when you are watching clips of CNN safely from your couch at home. But even though I spent some time on the "front lines" and "in person" in the literal sense, this critique applies to me too. Because as a white person, I was never really on the front line. Even when I was there physically, I can never know what it feels like to live in a weaponized body.

I was used to being an expert in so many areas. But I wasn't an expert on this. I didn't have more knowledge or experience in community organizing or direct action. And I most certainly didn't know better than Black organizers the best strategy for change or survival.

I had more personally at stake now that I was parenting a Black child. But I still had the privilege of the illusion of being able to walk away at any moment in a way that the Black folks in Ferguson did not. I was worried about my daughter. But I could go home. And I could take breaks.

The Black people in Ferguson and Black people all over the world do not get days off from being Black. White supremacy does not relent. I could leave Ferguson because I didn't live there. But for the people in Ferguson, this was their home. When we chanted "Whose streets? Our streets!" it wasn't rhetorical; those truly were their streets, the streets they knew, the streets they had grown up on, the streets they walked to grab a soda from the corner store or visit their grandma.

And even if there was somehow a way for these visionary Black activists to leave, there was nowhere to go. Anti-Blackness is a global phenomenon, and while the United States is steeped in a particularly toxic flavor of anti-Blackness, without complete liberation, there is nowhere in the world to go to escape. Because of this, and for so many other reasons, Black people have every incentive to get this right. This movement for Black Lives isn't a thought experiment for them. It is life and death.

Assuming that I knew better than Black people how to achieve their own goals of freedom was white supremacy at play.

I was a well-read white girl who cared about doing what was right. But the Black activists in the streets not only had good hearts and plenty of book knowledge; they also had grown up getting the "talk" about how to act around police. They grew up hearing stories passed down from their grandparents about navigating white supremacy. They felt these truths in their bodies; they could sense things I couldn't feel, notice things I couldn't see. No matter how many books I read filtered through my white gaze, many of these freedom fighters had read those books too, filtered through their own lived experiences. No matter how much I learned about MLK in my white suburban school, no matter how much head knowledge I thought I had about what movements might look like, I would never have the kind of gut-level, survival-based knowledge that comes with having the lived experience of dark skin.

I had to come to terms with the fact that just because I might not know what is going on in a particular moment doesn't necessarily mean that it is chaotic. Just because the current strategy wouldn't be my chosen strategy doesn't mean it's disorganized. Just because I don't have the details doesn't mean that they haven't been thought through meticulously. What it means is that I don't know. And sometimes that is OK, even necessary. My restlessness about not having access to every detail and plan is about my own need to feel in control of the situation.

Glennon Doyle's book *Untamed* teaches that love and control can't coexist. I thought that I wanted to control the narrative around the Ferguson protests out of love. I wanted them to be successful. I wanted them to be taken seriously. But Doyle tells us that love requires trust, and if we are trying to control something, we aren't trusting it, whether that's our partner, ourselves, or in my case, Black leaders of a liberation movement. My impulse to hold on so tightly, to control for the sake of my own narratives, my own values, my own comfort, had the potential to cause real damage. I needed to let go.

I wish I could tell you that I have overcome this compulsion for control, but I haven't. It is something that I am continuing to unlearn, often painfully. But it is necessary. This need for control isn't something that is merely individualized. The need for control is a part of white culture itself, something widespread and pervasive. It shows up every time a new viral hashtag pops up alerting us to the horrifying death of another Black person at the hands of the state. White people, who have never lived a single day of our lives under racialized oppression, fall all over ourselves on the internet about what the latest Black victim "should" have done to avoid being killed. The obsession with control is present any time white people try to tell Black people how to act, how to be, how to respond to their own oppression. The message is clear: know your place or die.

My faith tradition has a lot to say about control. We have an entire initiation ritual that is all about giving up our illusion of control. The rite of baptism in many Lutheran churches today involves a little bit of sprinkling, but sometimes I think the full-immersion folks are onto something. Going under the water, you have to hold your breath. Your chest gets tight. You come up out of the water with a gasp and a deep exhale, heavy, soaking robes floating around you.

Baptism, in Lutheran theology, is explained in stark terms. Baptism is dying and rising. We believe that there are parts of us that have to die daily so that new parts can rise up and be born. The moment a person is submerged in baptism is a moment of trust. You rely on the arms of the person baptizing you, believing that even though the ritual is designed to "drown" our sin, the person presiding over your baptism will not literally drown you. This action embodies surrender, the release of control.

This release is both terrifying and euphoric, which is how I find I experience most moments of liberation.

Baptism for Lutherans is not a singular event. It is an ongoing, lifelong journey that is complete only when our time on earth is over. I have experienced antiracism as a white person to be this way too. We are captive to the sin of white supremacy and cannot free ourselves. Racism is hundreds of years older than you or me. It is a web of lies and systems that was created for the benefit and protection of people like me, but it also acts as a suffocating trap for me and everyone else.

Like in baptism, we may be able to point to a single moment when we were initiated into this movement of antiracism, but it is the daily work of unlearning white supremacy, of dying to our internalized biases, that is the way to freedom. You might not have one single conversion moment you can point to. Perhaps there are many steps along the way that have affected you, people who have changed you, relationships that have formed you. It is not necessary to have some numinous experience to commit yourself to antiracism. While antiracism is radical, it is also quite ordinary in that it is most often made up of the day-to-day moments of life. Antiracism for white people can begin with things like personal and communal reflection on the internalized ideas of superiority we carry.

I thought that I knew what was best, but my need to control the movement in Ferguson was harmful. It was harmful to my relationships. It was harmful to the movement. It was harmful to me. It had to be released. It had to die for something new to be born in me.

We hold on to control because we think that control makes us safer. But it doesn't. The only way to safety and freedom is by uniting ourselves with Christ's death and resurrection and the crucified ones among us today. This means white Christians will have to be humble, acknowledging that we are not the experts we think we are. It means we have to silence our critiques of things we know nothing about. Solidarity includes sacrifice. It means that we have to loosen control of our resources, redistribute our stolen wealth, and even put our sense of financial stability on the line.

Antiracism is a daily dying and rising. Each day we have to unlearn old habits and shed old ways of being. Throughout most of recent history, the white church has stubbornly asserted ourselves at the center. Decentering whiteness means decentering white power, white culture, white values, white authority. It may very well mean the death of many of our structures and institutions. But it is only through this death that new life finds us.

Reflection Questions

1. Where have you felt the nudge of the Spirit lately in antioppression work?
2. How can your gifts benefit the antiracist body of Christ?
3. What part of protests makes you uncomfortable, and where do you feel this discomfort is rooted?
4. Elle writes about Lutheran baptism and the gift of daily dying and rising. For Elle, her tight grip of control is something that continually has to die for something new to be born. What has to die within you in order for something new to be born?
5. Elle writes, "Solidarity includes sacrifice. It means that we have to loosen control of our resources, redistribute our stolen wealth, and even put our sense of financial stability on the line." What comforts of white supremacy are you holding on to tightly?

Action Items

- If you are white, say yes to an invitation to visit a congregation of color or cultural event. Be intentional about decentering yourself, and make sure you let the hosts of this space steer. Give your offerings there, and release control of your resources.[4]
- Practice putting people over property; join a statewide campaign led by a Black Power organization or another people of color–led campaign to write to your representatives about reparations.
- In *Luther's Small Catechism*, Martin Luther said we ought to begin each day by remembering our baptismal identity: "In the morning, as soon as you get out of bed, you are to make the sign of the holy cross and say: 'God the Father, Son, and Holy Spirit watch over me. Amen.'"[5] Commit to this daily practice as a way to remember your baptismal identity as beloved by God and be empowered to your baptismal calling to renounce the evil of white supremacy. Pray throughout your day that God will protect you from the influence of white supremacy. Use your daily rituals of showering, brushing your teeth, or doing the dishes to ask God to drown the old sinful parts of our society and create something new and more just in its place.

3

TENSION

You have to tell the whole truth, the good and the bad, maybe some
things that are uncomfortable for some people.

—Representative John Lewis[1]

We white people love to think of ourselves as nice.

This is especially true of a certain brand of white people,
many of us middle class and hailing from the Midwest. We
pat ourselves on the back with pride for being [Your State
Here] nice. Where I grew up, in a state that is about 94 percent white and filled with Lutheran churches, we liked to
say we're "Iowa nice."

But too often, niceness is about convenience. It's about
our comfort. It's about control. It is our pathological desire
for niceness that leads white people to look at young Black
people crying out in the street and say,

"They should really say #AllLivesMatter."

"I'm all for protesting, but do they really have to
    inconvenience other people?"

"No one is going to listen to them if they are going to be
    so rude like that."

In other words, "Why can't they be nice?" A nice that is
tame, palatable, compliant, and always centers whiteness.
For white people and white culture, niceness is a false idol.
And it's a false idol with a body count. Yet when our Black
siblings are crying out, "Black Lives Matter!" we continue
to make human sacrifices to the altar of our bloodthirsty
god of niceness, caring more about our own comfort and
security than about children like Mike Brown dying in
the streets.

Body counts and blood sacrifices don't sound very nice.
But this kind of violence is a direct result of the dangerous
relationship between niceness and power—which always
finds a way to center itself on white ideals, white experiences, white feelings.

Most of us who are white live a life of unexamined privilege, and so the world seems at least mostly fair. Because we
don't experience systemic racial discrimination firsthand,
it's easy for us to assume that the world and its institutions are good or at least neutral. Most white people have a
worldview that the playing field is level, except for maybe in
a few isolated circumstances. But the truth is that the world
not only is *not* neutral but is in fact actively and aggressively
hostile toward people of color. There is a system in place
that has benefited me and people who look like me, and it's
been in place for hundreds of years.

A world wrapped in whiteness sees the Ferguson Uprising and the Movement for Black Lives as aggressive. We

don't see where this anger is coming from because we assume that our systems are good or at least neutral. And so we assume this anger is unprovoked. We don't see that what's truly aggressive is racism, that white supremacy started this fight, that the Movement for Black Lives and activists in Ferguson are acting out of self-defense against a system that would see Black people be annihilated before it would see them be free.

That doesn't sound nice. Because it's not. And because white people value niceness so much, when we hear the truth about our participation in a system that leads to widespread bloodshed and death, it's uncomfortable for us because it creates cognitive dissonance. And since we value our comfort above everything—even our Black siblings' lives—we try to find a way to make it not true. Any reminder of our participation in the violence of racism becomes the object of scorn and disbelief, and we will find any polite way to undermine it.

White people love niceness, but we fail to see that our ideas about polite society and civility are not very nice at all. They serve instead to preserve a system that is criminalizing people of color and dehumanizing white people with our callous indifference. They act to protect institutions built on killing the bodies of people of color to the detriment of our own souls.

These ideas about niceness and civility are more things that needed to die in me as part of this baptism into new life. They are things I struggle with still that have to die within me every day in order for me to be transformed, for something better to be reborn.

I am writing this in June 2020 in the midst of an uprising throughout the nation and even around the world. This week I was with a group of white progressive church people as we organized our response to more and more murders of Black people by law enforcement in our country. Our group hemmed and hawed about how we might get involved in this current moment. Some people wanted to try reasoning with individual police officers. I mentioned that the stated goal of Black liberation organizations in our city was for the total abolition of policing as we know it, that SOUL (the group I organize with in Chicago's South Side), Black Lives Matter Chicago, Black Youth Project 100, and Assata's Daughter all have explicit abolitionist stances.

I proposed that the people most affected by police violence should get to set the agenda and that these organizations had been consistently working toward abolition for years. Some of the white people in that group became visibly uncomfortable at the mention of abolition. That is when my niceness took over. It is no secret that I am an abolitionist. But in that moment, I was afraid to break the code of whiteness and say something. I saw the tension, and I was afraid to raise more. What I *wanted* to say, what was screaming inside of me, was, "I have Black teenagers. This is not a fucking game to me." What I actually said was nothing, and then I stewed with anger, guilt, and regret. I could have used this opportunity to have a difficult but important conversation with someone who shares my values, someone I care about. But I was more worried about coming off too militant, too angry, not nice enough. So I kept what I was feeling inside. I let this conditioned response of niceness get in the way of my actual values. Because although I sometimes fail to act accordingly, I don't actually value "niceness" at all.

White people use niceness and civility dishonestly. We say we value niceness, but what we really value is being in charge of what niceness looks like and when it's appropriate by our own standards. We are addicted to control.

We say we value niceness, but we look away when the state, with our tax dollars and on our behalf, is slaughtering our siblings. We value "security."

We say we value niceness, but we silence anyone who dissents to the genocide of white supremacy. We value "peace."

We say we value niceness, but we find chants fueled with anger to be distasteful, cries punctuated with curse words to be vulgar, disregarding the true vulgarity: blood in our streets, murders committed on our behalf. We value "propriety."

We say we value niceness, but we criticize the honest expressions of people who have grown up with unspeakable generational trauma. We sit comfortably removed from the embodied reality of their pain and critique the tone with which they tell us the truth. We value "civility."

We say we value niceness, but this kind of niceness isn't kindness or compassion or accompaniment or self-sacrifice. It's not Christ's example of emptying ourselves for the sake of the other.[2] It's the opposite—silencing and oppressing the other for the sake of ourselves.

We say we value niceness, but the truth is that we care more about being polite and comfortable than we care about liberation. We are worshipping at the altar of niceness instead of following the cross of Christ. This is an abuse of priorities that is abhorrent to the God who introduces Herself[3] over and over as the one who brought us "out of the house of slavery."[4]

I saw whiteness's multiple attempts to enforce niceness through militarized force in Ferguson and St. Louis. White people in cars were so angry about blocked traffic that they tried to run over protesters. These were the same people who would label actions like disrupting traffic as "violent."

The police would punish protesters for our lack of "niceness" by kettling us and then tear-gassing us.[5] It wasn't about public safety; it was about coercively establishing control to keep our message from getting out. This is why the police in Ferguson tried to secure "media zones" to hide away journalists, why they tear-gassed people with cameras, harassed livestreamers, and arrested reporters. They had a vested interest in controlling the narrative to keep the truth from getting out.

Officers targeted places known for supporting the Movement for Black Lives, like MoKaBe's, which was tear-gassed without warning. MoKaBe's is a radical coffee shop in the Tower Grove neighborhood of St. Louis. The owner, Mo, is a gay woman about my mom's age who established MoKaBe's a couple of decades back so there would be places for LGBTQIA+ people to gather and socialize outside of gay bars. The walls are full of protest signs, and stickers decorate the front of the appliances behind the counter.

You might see people gathered there for community meetings or staging before a protest. When Gynnya McMillen was killed in a youth detention center in Kentucky in January 2016, my comrade Alicia Street and I organized some solidarity efforts, including one at MoKaBe's. After the grand jury had failed to indict Darren Wilson, the Ferguson Action Network reported that there were actions in over 175 cities in solidarity with the protesters in Ferguson and Mike's family. We remembered how the protests and actions across the nation encouraged us and helped sustain us in a time when we felt so desperate and defeated, and we wanted to give that kind of support to other cities full of young, first-time activists resisting state violence. So we organized an event near Valentine's Day to make "Activist Love Letters" for the protesters in Kentucky. We held that event at MoKaBe's. They even provided the construction paper, markers, and supplies.

Games sit on the open shelves at MoKaBe's for customers to take down and play. They serve brunch on Sundays with amazing stuffed French toast. On my birthday, Mo's son John made me my signature drink and stuck a candle in it, and everyone sang to me. My daughter Alice would wander around making friends with everyone, and the workers would let her help with little tasks like bussing tables and then slip her a ten-dollar bill. That's the kind of place MoKaBe's is.

During the Ferguson Uprising, particularly in the fall of 2014, MoKaBe's was a designated safe place where people could come inside to use the bathroom, get a drink of water, or rest. The police tear-gassed it. Video footage shows police dropping multiple canisters into the enclosed area right outside full of people seeking safety from the rubber bullets the police had been firing in the streets.[6] Tear-gas canisters were recovered from inside the building itself. People in MoKaBe's that night included workers from organizations like Amnesty International who had been active in publicly holding the police accountable for their militarized violence against the public.

MoKaBe's wasn't attacked by the police despite being a place of refuge.

It was attacked because of it.

I saw the same people who condemned the "violence" of protests defend actions like this by the police. White culture pretends to idolize nonviolence because it seems nice and civil, but in reality, whiteness uses nonviolence as a shield to avoid dealing with the racist systemic violence already present in our society. We are typically OK with demonstrations as long as they don't inconvenience us or interfere with our routine in any way. As long as they don't cause a traffic jam or make us late for an appointment (although we seem totally fine with traffic due to a sports event or streets blocked off for parades).

White people defend state violence because it protects our access to the status quo and our own comfort, void of the tense truths about the reality of the suffering of our Black siblings. The reason many white people have trouble thinking of nonviolent direct action as truly nonviolent is that it is disruptive by nature, and that doesn't feel very nice.

It's not supposed to be nice.

Direct action intentionally interrupts our daily flow and rhythm in an attempt to raise tension. This tension isn't new. It isn't being created out of thin air. It has always existed for our siblings of color.

For people of color and other oppressed people, the tension caused by marginalization is ever present with very real consequences. Medical professionals say that the stress caused by racism, for example, is a major factor contributing to the disparities in health for people of color.[7] Racism is like being force-fed a poison. Direct action is what happens when people refuse to drink that poison and instead bring a bottle of it to the doorstep of those force-feeding them and demand that they gaze upon the reality of it.

Direct action doesn't create *new* tension. It redistributes the tension *that is already there* and puts it back where it belongs—at the source.

Many people—white people, in particular—have little tolerance for tension. We have been taught to avoid tension. Our conditioning has trained us to recoil from discomfort, to think of it as an inherently bad thing, something to sidestep and evade at all costs. Instead of leaning into tension to see what we can learn from it, we often avoid it. But when we do this, when we turn away from tension, we fail to see the gift that this tension can be in revealing the truth. We miss out on the clarity it brings with it, the opportunity to move forward.

Dr. Martin Luther King Jr. wrote about the way "peace" is weaponized by the status quo in his famous "Letter from a Birmingham Jail." He talked about the difference between what he called "negative peace," or an absence of tension, and "positive peace which is the presence of justice."[8]

So often those in support of the status quo shame inconveniences, like roads blocked by protesters, by calling them "violent" because they have confused peace with a lack of discomfort. It's why white supremacy paints the righteous anger of Black people as threatening or nonpeaceful—because it's uncomfortable for white people, and discomfort (or inconvenience or change) doesn't fit this watered-down idea of "peace." Calling protesters "violent" is another way to exert control, to try to tarnish their cause in the eyes of popular imagination and discredit it. Because white people value civility so much, whiteness has cast Black people throughout history as "uncivilized," as the enemies of peace, to avoid accountability.

Before the grand jury failed to indict Darren Wilson for Michael Brown's murder in November 2014, the atmosphere in Missouri was tense, and the officials in Missouri made calls for peace. The Democratic governor, Jay Nixon, declared a state of emergency and sent in the National Guard.

Many activists and community leaders rightly critiqued these actions, saying that for Black people in Missouri, there has been a "state of emergency" for a long time. White supremacy has caused an ongoing, racialized state of emergency for much of the population of Missouri.

So.

Where was the declaration of a state of emergency when segregation in St. Louis meant that your quality of life could vary drastically from your neighbor just across Delmar Boulevard? Where was the state of emergency when majority-Black public schools, like Mike's, lost their accreditation? Where was the state of emergency when there was a thirty-five-year life expectancy discrepancy between people living in the Black and white parts of the city?[9] How can we call the normal way our lives are structured "peaceful" and want to get back to this "peace" if it means continuing a true (and silent) state of emergency for our neighbors?

As God said to the prophet Jeremiah, "They have treated the wound of my people carelessly, saying, 'Peace, peace,' when there is no peace."[10] When white authorities call for "peace" in the midst of protests like the ones in Ferguson, they aren't calling for the deep peace that comes only with justice that MLK references. They are calling for a return to white comfort and business as usual; they are calling for an end to tension without acknowledging that Black communities ravaged by state violence and lack of access to education, health care, and social services have experienced a lack of peace for a long, long time.

This abuse of the word *peace* is why some people call the strategy of direct action *militant nonviolent resistance*; the powers that be and the state have so often co-opted the word *peace* and watered it down to mean "nice" or "accommodating." By that definition of *peace*, the protests were not peaceful. They were meant to raise tension, to get people's attention.

A popular chant in the streets of Ferguson as well as at other demonstrations throughout the country has this refrain: "No justice, no peace."

White people tended to take that statement as a threat by mentally inserting a conditional "if-then" statement:

if you do not give us the justice we seek, *then* we will destroy your peace. That is how I used to hear it too. And for some Black people, it may mean that, and that feeling is more than justified.

But for the Black folks I met in the streets, this chant is less of a threat than a statement of reality. This became real for me when I saw Mike Brown Sr. wearing a shirt that has the words "No justice, no peace" framing a sweet photo of Michael as a baby. The meaning was written in heartbreak all over his father's face:

If there is no justice, there can be no peace.
This lack of justice has brought on a lack of peace.
Unless there is justice, how can we be at peace?

The state wages a particular propaganda campaign by calling anything that disrupts the status quo "violent." But the militant nonviolent strategy that MLK and Jesus employed was not about accommodation or comfort. It was full of tensions and disruption and confrontation and challenge. Nonviolence at its core is rooted in love. And sometimes the most loving thing to do is to put up boundaries, to love yourself and others by refusing to allow others to harm you. Jesus outlines a way of resistance that reclaims human dignity and demands accountability. This way is not passive. It is active and courageous and engaged. It was dangerous enough to get him killed.

I am committed to militant nonviolent resistance. This commitment is something that I struggle with daily. Dedicating oneself to nonviolence is a decision people have to make for themselves; it is not a decision that people with power or privilege can make for oppressed people. That is not nonviolence. It is repression. It is inherently violent for white people to critique the methods that Black people use to get free. I do not make a commitment to nonviolence for myself out of a sense of moral superiority. I think freedom, by any means necessary, is as much of a moral imperative as peace. I am committed to nonviolence because when I look at the US empire, I recognize that they will always outspend and outarm us. And so we have to be more resilient and more creative. And liberation movements have always been rife with resilience and creativity. Storytellers, musicians, and artists are some of the most powerful weapons against oppression. This is why fascist regimes often threaten and target artists. Creativity is powerful.

In Ferguson during the Uprising, some people used to carry full-length mirrors to the riot line. A group of artists even made a coffin out of mirrors to carry to the protests.[11] The website for the project explains, "With an aim to evoke reflection and empathy for the deaths of young people of color who have lost their lives unjustly in the United States and worldwide, the . . . Mirror Casket was performed as part of a 'Funeral Procession of Justice' during the Ferguson October protests. As community members carried it from the site of Michael Brown's death to the police department of the community, its mirrors challenged viewers to look within and see their reflections as both whole and shattered, as both solution and problem, as both victim and aggressor."[12]

We used to say that the militarized police force looked like Robocops. It was dehumanizing for us to be on the receiving side of their violence, but it also quite literally dehumanized them by making them look nonhuman with their armor, vests, shields, helmets, and armored vehicles physically separating them from us. And people would bring these full-length mirrors as a tactic of resistance, to raise tension by telling the truth about what the police were doing by holding up their reflection to them. I saw the artists process the mirrored casket through the streets during Ferguson October, a weekend of resistance in 2014. As they neared the riot line with the armored police, one woman collapsed to her knees in tears. Members of the crowd stared expectantly at the police, at their multiple reflections in the shattered mirror, at their own image. The mirrors made the scene even grimmer. Officers shifted their weight, set their jaws, and looked straight forward, trying to avoid making eye contact with their own reflection.

This is the key strategy of direct action. It redistributes tension by taking the risk of telling the truth out loud and in public. It is honest about things we would rather avoid. It is the pure, stark truth we have tried to cover up.

My journey into antiracism has been full of mirrors like this. So much had to be unveiled in my own life. And a lot of the unveiling was the result of having mirrors held up to me and being uncomfortable with what I saw. I too felt the urge to avert my eyes. I was so attached to thinking of myself as "one of the good ones" that I was often unaware of the ways that even that line of thinking centered whiteness. I needed to be shown the ways that my own worship of niceness, civility, tone policing, and respectability were getting in the way. Just like my need for control, my attachment to these things had to die too.

Throughout Ferguson and St. Louis, white people undertook a targeted effort to discredit the Uprising and the Movement for Black Lives. They would smile and say, "*All* lives matter." Or they would promote public relations–type campaigns about how great Ferguson is, a way to distance themselves from the truths laid bare in Ferguson by saying, "This isn't who we are."

But the protests—and the response to the protests—were a mirror that showed us the truth: this *is* who we are. We are a community captive to racism. We are a country founded on stolen land and stolen labor that continues to exploit Black people for the benefit of white people, and we use the militarized arm of the state to violently suppress anyone who fights back against it. We *are* a country where unarmed Black teenage kids are killed by armed white police who demonize them in the press. We can't say this sort of thing doesn't happen here; we can't say that this is an anomaly.

We can't keep hiding the truth about who we are because it's uncomfortable.

The Lutheran sacrament of baptism includes what are known as the "renunciations." This is a time of radical, often uncomfortable honesty and resistance. Before we are asked as a community to affirm what we believe, we are first asked to renounce the devil, the powers of this world, and the ways of sin. Before we say the Apostles' Creed, before the water, before anything else, we have to sit in the tension of the commitment we are making to resist evil.

Before we can tell the truth about what we believe, we have to name the lies for what they are.

Talking about the devil can be tense for a lot of white Lutherans, but just as God shows up contextually in different ways for different times and places, evil manifests differently depending on context too. Evil and the devil go by many names. One of them is the "Father of Lies," which is what Jesus calls the devil in John 8. Another one is "white supremacy"—a dangerous, murderous lie from the devil that has a stronghold in the hearts of white people and white institutions, including the church. In our baptisms, when we renounce the devil and the forces that defy God, we are also called to renounce white supremacy.

For white people, that means acknowledging our part in it instead of hiding from it because we fear how tense it makes us feel. When we do this, when we welcome the tension that the truth brings with it, we can move forward. We don't get to skip right to the part at the end where the congregation applauds to welcome the newly baptized. We have to experience the difficult, uncomfortable parts first. It is only when we tell the truth, when we renounce the lies, when we die to sin that we can rise again to new life.

Reflection Questions

1. What definition of *violence* did you grow up with? Who benefits from this definition?
2. What does true, lasting peace look like, smell like, feel like, and taste like? Have you ever experienced a glimpse of this peace? Name a situation in your own life where evil was dispatched and justice reigned, even just for a moment.
3. Who are the peacemakers in your community? What organizations or leaders dig below the surface to manifest true and lasting peace?
4. What have you been taught about tension and discomfort? What does tension feel like in your body?
5. In what ways have you mistaken discomfort for danger? How can you welcome tension as a gift?
6. What behaviors or patterns of living are you complacent in that are evil and that you need to renounce?

Action Items

- Prepare yourself to make some people in your circles tense with difficult but necessary conversations. Call out your racist family member this Thanksgiving. Make people who have told a racist joke or made a racist comment uncomfortable in your workplace. This work within our families/jobs or careers/circles often feels most risky, but it is most important.
- Reflect with your pastor and a group in your church on the behaviors and beliefs from which you need to communally renounce and repent. Work together to write a liturgy of confession to be used in worship.

4

THE STAKES

If the Christian church in the 21st century does not dismantle white supremacy, there will be no Christian witness in 50 years in this country.

—Pastor Lenny Duncan[1]

During the Uprising, I posted what I was seeing and experiencing on Twitter and Facebook. Social media felt like a way to get information to the people in my circles, and most importantly, I was more able to amplify the voices often left out of mainstream conversations about race and current events.

Part of me felt a responsibility to share the story because so often, I saw misinformation being spread around by people that I knew. I saw one photo of my friend Jermell Hasson holding a protest sign that had been doctored. Besides the obvious Photoshop job, I knew right away because I had seen the sign in person. It said, "No Mother Should Have to Fear for Her Son's Life Every Time He Leaves Home. #blacklivesmatter #stayhuman."

Someone edited the sign to say instead, "No Mother Should Have to Fear for Her Son's Life Every Time He Robs a Store."

This racist Photoshop was referencing some disputed events before Mike Brown's death. Under pressure to release the name of Mike's killer, the Ferguson police chief, Thomas Jackson, also released stills of security footage from a convenience store earlier that day. The footage was released against the advice of the Department of Justice[2] and was a clear attempt to smear Mike's character and justify the officer's excessive use of force by insinuating that Mike had committed a robbery before he was killed. The accusation that Mike committed a robbery has been contested, for example, in Jason Pollock's documentary, *Stranger Fruit*. Whatever Mike did or didn't do was definitely not a capital crime worthy of death. Regardless of what happened that morning, Mike had a right as a human being to tell his side of the story, to explain what happened. If he was ever formally charged with a crime, Mike had a right to defend himself in front of a jury of his peers. And he will never get to do that because he was killed by the police.

Police Chief Jackson later admitted that Mike wasn't stopped because he was a robbery suspect. He was stopped for walking in the street, for jaywalking. Now every time I cross the road, I think about how walking in the street became a death sentence for a teenage boy.

If you are Black in America, any perceived slight can mean you're subject to death by our state-sanctioned firing squads. Whether you are selling loose cigarettes like Eric Garner, forgetting to use your turn signal like Sandra Bland, shopping at Walmart like John Crawford III, or playing in the park like Tamir Rice, any misstep—or imagined misstep—can get you killed. Stories like Aiyana Mo'Nay Stanley Jones or Terence Crutcher or Breonna Taylor show that if you are Black, even if you are in your own home, you are not safe from intruders in blue uniforms who will murder you and then walk free.

White people often say things like "If [insert Black victim here] had just complied, this wouldn't have happened." We place so much emphasis on picking apart the victim while holding no standard approaching basic decency for the armed agents of the state whose vehicles are emblazoned with the message "Protect and Serve." We expect everyday civilians to be calm and accommodate the fear of jumpy, trigger-happy police officers instead of holding accountable the officers who we have trained, paid, and given special authority. Someone created that racist meme of my friend Jermell to justify Mike's death and to discredit the protests. They thought that the Ferguson Uprising was ridiculous, that Mike deserved to die, and they altered the image to reinforce a message of lynching logic as old as white supremacy itself: stay in your place.

Someone edited that photo. And then thousands of people shared it.

One of the people who shared the doctored image was a white woman named Cindy, someone from the church I had attended and worked at before moving to Missouri. When I saw it in my newsfeed, I felt the wind go out of me. This was someone I had worshipped with every Sunday. We held hands to say the Lord's Prayer. We gathered around the Lord's table and broke bread together. With tears in my eyes, I commented on the picture about how disappointed I was that she would share something so obviously altered and so racist. I said I knew Jermell, that he was genuine and sweet. I shared my fear about the way that this meme made him a target.

Cindy was defensive. She told me she couldn't believe I would call her racist when she had supported the adoption of my Black daughter. Then she unfriended me.

I learned from that interaction that white people can—and often do—support "missions" abroad to places like Sierra Leone, West Africa, or transracial adoption and still harbor ideas of racialized superiority. White people with loved ones who are people of color, whether through interracial relationships or adoptions, are not exempt from racism. In fact, white adoptive parents often use our children of color as props to explain why we "aren't racist." The transracial adoption system and the adoption process is a business steeped in racism. The ethics of transracial adoption are complex, and as a parent of Black children, I have made many mistakes. Our proximity to people of color does not absolve us of our racism—not our individual internalized biases or our participation in racist systems.

I'd seen some of the ways that white people like to think of ourselves as saviors when I spent time in Sierra Leone. I have participated in this thinking. When white-led nonprofits and nongovernmental agencies have a disproportionate amount of power compared to the local people, it re-creates neocolonialist policies and practices that disempower people and cause lasting harm.

This is true in Sierra Leone, but it is also true more broadly, including in the United States. In the past few years, I have learned more about the ways that churches and the nonprofit sector, sometimes rightfully called the *nonprofit industrial complex*, participate in white supremacy. Well-meaning white liberals often head organizations meant to "help" others without doing the important power

analysis and redistribution of resources necessary for liberation. This creates a top-down approach and a rift between
people with privilege and people who have been oppressed
and exploited. White people often invest in nonprofits
as a way to prove our own goodness and to assuage our
white guilt. Cindy believed that because she had written
a check for the digging of a new well I helped coordinate
in Sierra Leone and because she helped support the adoption of my daughter, she could share racist memes without
any accountability. She thought she could buy my silence,
that her money made her a good person, and that she was
entitled to share whatever harmful images she wanted. She
believed the same lies I had been taught growing up, that
racists were monsters and well-meaning white people who
do "nice" things can't possibly be racist.

It hurt a lot. But this wouldn't be the first or last time
that I would lose a friend because I wouldn't excuse their
racism. I noticed a particular phenomenon: people would
"like" pictures of my Black daughter, cheesing for the
camera with a big fluffy bow on top of her head, but would
be silent or—even worse—outright racist when it came to
her liberation. My mom's friends, people who had watched
me grow up, would see me post about Ferguson and would
parrot responses about the "violence" of protesters, making
excuses for the violence of police. I felt a growing seed of
dread inside me as I realized that my Black daughter would
not be seven forever. One day she would be a teenager. One
day they wouldn't think of her as adorable. One day they
could see her as a threat.

In February 2014, as part of an annual Black History
Month celebration, activist Ruby Sales came to Christ
Church Cathedral, which housed the office where I worked
for the bishop. Ruby Sales was a young activist in the civil

rights era during the Freedom Rides. She became well known after the death of white Episcopal seminarian Jonathan Daniels. Daniels was shot with a shotgun by a special county deputy in the act of shielding seventeen-year-old Sales, saving her life.

When Ruby Sales, affectionately called Mother Ruby by many in the movement, visited the cathedral, she spoke about the Spirithouse Project, a civil rights organization that, among other things, sheds light on state violence against Black people. I came into this event believing that police brutality against Black people was real but not understanding its scope or seriousness. Mother Ruby told me stories about police violence I had never heard before. She told us about Chavis Carter, for example, a young man who was found dead, handcuffed in the back of a police car. The story the police told was that he somehow had a gun on him (despite the fact that the police searched him twice) and that he shot himself while handcuffed. Sales quoted suffragist and antilynching activist Ida B. Wells: "Those who commit the murders write the reports."[3]

My mind was spinning. I looked at Alice sitting next to me and felt I might burst into tears or throw up.

After Sales spoke, she graciously offered her time for a question-and-answer and discussion period. I raised my hand to ask a question. I was wondering how to work through this tension I was feeling. On the one hand, as a parent of a Black child, I had been told by Black parents how important it is to teach my Black children how to interact with police. To "do all the right things," to be polite, to say "Yes, sir," to make no sudden movements, to comply no matter what. That this is what would keep her safe, this is what would protect her, this is what would keep her alive. On the other hand, somewhere inside of me, I knew that I wanted to raise my Black child to be proud, to stand up for herself, and to resist white supremacy and its agents. I wanted my child to be free. I asked Ruby Sales how to navigate this tension—how to keep my Black child safe but also how to preserve her dignity and her spirit.

As she began to answer, the spirit of Black, queer poet and activist Audre Lorde entered the room through the voice of Ruby Sales. Sales reminded me of all of the stories of Black people who did everything right and were still not safe from racialized violence in our racist society. She quoted Lorde, saying, "Your silence will not protect you," and told me that this narrative I was presenting was a false choice: that teaching our Black children to stand up and fight back *was* the only way to keep them safe, by building the kind of world where they can thrive.

A courageous statement like this could only come with integrity from someone like Ruby Sales, who had survived an attempt on her life while organizing for the civil rights movement. It is not as if Sales said this glibly. She is well aware of the dangers, more than most people.

Almost exactly six months later, unarmed Black teenager Michael Brown was shot and killed, igniting an uprising that would blossom into a movement. This moment with Lorde through Sales prepared me to be a part of this movement and to be the kind of parent my revolutionary daughter would need me to be by allowing her to be a part of it too. Throughout the rest of my time in St. Louis during the Ferguson Uprising, I saw how important Audre Lorde and other radical artists and leaders were to the Black activists facing down armored vehicles and tear gas and rubber bullets night after night. I saw leaders, most of them women or nonbinary, many of them queer, conjure her up with their words, quoting her poetry like incantations to speak her spirit into existence. Instead of modeling themselves after Dr. Martin Luther King Jr., a Christian man who was radical but had been whitewashed and domesticated over time in the memory of dominant white culture, these young leaders called upon the names of elders like Assata Shakur and Angela Davis and upon the memory and legacy of ancestors like Ella Baker and Audre Lorde.

These historic leaders and elders made it clear what was at stake for Black people in this movement. The young Black activists would lead chants (and teach Alice to lead chants too) quoting a letter by Assata Shakur that made it clear that there was no other option but total liberation:

> It is our duty to fight for our freedom.
> It is our duty to win.
> We must love and support each other.
> We have nothing to lose but our chains.[4]

I was gaining clarity about why Black liberation mattered to me because I began to feel some of the fear that Black mothers had been feeling for hundreds of years. This movement wasn't just important because of some abstract idea about "the right thing to do." It wasn't some thought exercise or self-improvement project. This was my daughter. My sweet, silly, feisty daughter. Now that my other daughter, Jessica, is here in the United States with me, I parent two Black children who are more precious to me than life itself. I would do anything to keep them safe, but even more importantly, I would do anything to make them *free*.

But even though my children are my main motivating factor in this work, I'm also motivated by my own need to lose my chains.

When I was in Ferguson, I started noticing an eerie similarity between the way that people talked about Michael Brown and some of my own experiences. As a survivor of sexual abuse and assault and dating violence, I had experienced the phenomenon of *victim blaming* too many times to count. The way that people began to talk about Mike, to condemn him, to make him responsible for his own death felt *triggering*.

When I heard white people make jokes like "He should pull up his pants," I remembered "What were you wearing?"

It sounded a lot like "Her skirt was too short."

When I heard them say "He shouldn't have been in the street," I remembered "What did you expect, being out at night?"

It sounded a lot like "She shouldn't have been walking alone."

When I heard "He should've just complied," I remembered "Look what you made me do."

It sounded a lot like "She was asking for it."

Black men and white women have a complicated history. White supremacy has often pitted us against each other, and white women frequently align ourselves with white supremacy in hopes that it will offer us some sort of access to power and protection. We saw this in the 2016 presidential election and again in 2020, where the majority of white women voted against their own interest for Donald Trump, a misogynist, because they were so committed to the ways his racism protected their whiteness. Another historic example is the death of teenager Emmett Till, who was blamed for his horrific lynching because a white woman said he was flirting with her. She confessed decades later that this was a lie.[5] A more recent example is the story of Amy Cooper in the spring of 2020, a white woman who had her dog off a leash in Central Park in New York City. When a Black man named Christian Cooper (no relation) tried to ask her to leash her dog so that he could continue bird-watching, she called the police on him and pretended that he was threatening her life. Amy Cooper knew this history of racialized violence and weaponized the police in order to teach a Black man his place.[6]

Because of these stories and so many others like them, Black men (and Black people in general) are often wary of white women—and for good reason. White women have propped up white supremacy throughout history. I have done this too. I have been socialized to think of Black and Brown men as a threat. I have prioritized my own experiences over theirs. This is a notable failure on my part and on the part of white women morally. But it is also a failure strategically because of the threads of similarity between cisheteropatriarchy and white supremacy. The same victim blaming that tore Mike apart in the media would tarnish our names too. Instead of allowing these systems to divide us, white women have a particular stake in being in solidarity with Black victims of state violence, noting that Black women and Black nonbinary people have particular wisdom to offer as people who experience both white supremacist state violence and gender-based oppression. We will not end gender-based violence without ending white supremacy.

Sometimes people ask me how I can be a police and prison abolitionist as a survivor of dating violence and sexual violence. Our imaginations have been so limited that we often think the carceral system is the only avenue for justice. But for me, the carcel system in our country that killed Michael

Brown and locks up tons of poor Black and Brown people throughout this country isn't justice. It doesn't make me safer. This system traumatizes and abuses people, creating more and more victims. Sexual assault is not uncommon in prison, even if it is vastly underreported, and my convictions as a feminist and survivor tell me that absolutely *no one* deserves that kind of abuse.

The overpolicing of Black men in particular is often justified by narratives propping up the purity of white womanhood, as if Black men are inherently predatory and white women are princesses who have to be defended and protected. We incarcerate Black men to keep them safely locked away from white women. I am sick of having my body objectified like this as leverage for a racist system. I refuse to let white supremacy capitalize on my most painful stories to inflict pain on Black people. This narrative is devastating to the Black and Brown bodies it seeks to control, but it harms and exploits me too. Because, to paraphrase Indigenous artist and activist Lilla Watson, our liberation is bound up together. None of us are free until all of us are free.

In addition to the intertwining relationship of white supremacy and the cisheteropatriarchy (along with capitalism), there are other things at stake for me and all white people in ending white supremacy.

Even for the police.

When I was first arrested amid a demonstration at the police station during Ferguson October, it was raining so hard and there were so many of us that they had issues processing all of us. Partially because of the chaos and partially because of my own white privilege, I was able to keep my backpack with me when they put me in the back of a police van with other demonstrators. With the help of the others, I was able to contort my body enough to get out my phone and live-tweet my arrest and take a selfie of my handcuffs.

Matt Pearce, a journalist from the *Los Angeles Times*, tweeted at me asking to do an interview. Pearce was one of a handful of national news reporters I had trusted to report accurately throughout the Ferguson Uprising (the other two were Ryan Reilly and Wesley Lowery, who were arrested by the Ferguson police the first week after Mike's death). I agreed to do the interview, and he asked why I was there.

I tweeted back, "I'm here out of a deep love for both Black youth and police officers. We all deserve a better system as children of God. Black lives matter. We stand [with you] & won't stop til it's better. We love you."

I still feel that way. People often think I hate cops. I hate policing. But being up close with them so often at the riot line and during arrests has reminded me of their humanity underneath all of that riot gear. I am angry with police officers and the system of policing. But I see also the way that this system is harming them too.

At the riot line, you have to pay close attention to what the police are doing, notice their movements, because things can change in an instant. A protest that seems fairly calm can become escalated by the police in seconds. I got a lot of practice observing police for the sake of my own safety but even more for the sake of the safety of the Black people there with me. When police were particularly agitated, activists would call white people to the front of the line because the cops were much less likely to hurt a line of white people. Often our faces were only a few inches apart.

I have a distinct memory from that fall of a line of police in front of us. They were wearing padding and helmets and holding clubs. I looked down at the officer in front of me and noticed his leg was jiggling. He was practically jumping out of his skin. I thought, *He doesn't want to be here either.* I realized that just like *I* would rather be at home watching Netflix with my spouse on the couch, he would probably rather do the same thing.

They changed formation. Another white police officer was in front of me. I looked into his eyes, darting from side to side. He looked so, so young. He exhaled a short, nervous breath. I smelled something that seemed familiar to me. Was that vodka? Definitely some kind of alcohol.

I said earlier that the police looked like Robocops, and it's true. They did not look human; they were literally dehumanized, separated from us, their neighbors, by shields and armored vehicles. Their actions and participation in this system dehumanized us. But it also cut them off from their own humanity.

I want to make clear that I am not suggesting we should center white police officers in the quest for Black liberation. This is an explanation of the ways that the roles of oppressed and oppressor are harmful to everyone, but we should not pretend that this means they are harmful in the same way or to the same degree. This is also not a plea for respectability or permission to tone-police people who have been hurt by authorities when they express their pain. "Fuck the police" can be a righteous, prophetic statement not unlike "You brood of vipers!" or other harsh words from the prophets aimed at those who destroy communities and harm the vulnerable.

At the same time, sometimes white progressives use a hatred of police as a way to distance ourselves from them. We like to pretend that we are not somehow a part of the same system, that we are the "good ones." It is another way of demonizing racists with caricatures to obscure the fact that they are not that much different than us. They are us. In recognizing our shared humanity with the police, we can also be honest about our shared culpability.

People of color are losing their lives. We lose our humanity. This is what is at risk for white people if we refuse to actively dismantle white supremacy. It is not enough to be passively "nonracist." Author and psychologist Beverly Daniel Tatum explains this in her book on racial identity development, *Why Are All the Black Kids Sitting Together in the Cafeteria?* She writes,

> I sometimes visualize the ongoing cycle of racism as a moving walkway at the airport. Active racist behavior is the equivalent to walking fast on the conveyor belt. . . . Passive racist behavior is equivalent to standing still on the walkway. No overt effort is being made, but the conveyor belt moves the bystanders along to the same destination as those who are actively walking. Some of the bystanders may feel the motion of the conveyor belt, see the active racists ahead of them and choose to turn around. . . . But unless they are walking actively in the opposite direction at a speed faster than the conveyor belt—unless they are actively antiracist—they will find themselves carried along with the others.[7]

The script of white supremacy in our culture is so entrenched that without intentional effort, even well-meaning white people are swept along with it. And this passiveness allows this system to brutalize our siblings of color, doing harm to our own souls.

When our siblings are not free, we are not free either, because, as with the example of my own experiences of sexual violence, our liberation is tied to one another. But we are also not free because we are limited and damaged by being in the role of the oppressor, by allowing violence to be committed on our behalf.

The effects of white supremacy on white people and people of color are very different. Make no mistake, the true targets of white supremacy are people of color. But the stakes are high for all of us in different ways.

The white church has often been afraid to speak out against white supremacy and racialized capitalism. This is in part because of our indoctrination into white niceness and our worship of idols like civility and control. But it is also because the white church in general has been cowardly in the face of risk. With a few notable and courageous exceptions, history has shown that on the whole, white faith leaders have either propped up white supremacy or chosen to remain silent in the face of anti-Blackness and most other forms of oppression. Often the choice to remain silent is due to what is perceived to be an overwhelming amount of risk. Church leaders who speak on public events, especially speaking on particular instances of white supremacy like the murder of Michael Brown, risk losing church members. Losing members means losing funding, leading to a loss of jobs and livelihood. With the decline of Christendom, the institutionalized power of the church is dwindling, and these anxieties are already at the front of every church leader's mind. We fear losing public (i.e., white) support (i.e., money). We worry about our already tenuous influence and standing within the community.

White church leaders are often overwhelmed by these risks and then choose not to engage in the important work of antiracism. What many church leaders fail to recognize—and what I often still forget—is that *remaining silent is not without risk*. We think going along with the status quo will protect us. But just as Mother Ruby Sales said to me, quoting Audre Lorde, "Your silence will not protect you." The risks of the inaction of the white church in response to racial injustice are costly. Neutrality is a lie. Even if it feels safer, the risk of our silence is higher than the risk of action.

The most important risk is the loss of life of the beloved Black and Brown and Indigenous people made in the image of God. And when white people are complicit in systems that perpetuate this violence against our siblings of color, we weaken our connection to the God that created them and we deaden our own souls.

For the church, our ongoing failure to keep the vows we made at baptism to testify to God's liberating love for all people puts our public witness at risk. We believe that Jesus Christ chose to limit his godly privilege for the sake of humanity. When he chose to do this, he also chose to come to Earth enfleshed as a dark-skinned Palestinian Jew, born to an unwed teenage mother in an occupied land under the terror of the reign of the Roman Empire. This empire would be the very thing to kill him, lynching him as an insurrectionist, hanging his body high for all to see.

His resurrection was defiance in the face of this empire.

Today, if we do not act with each breath to tear down every vestige of the death cult of white supremacy, we betray the gospel of Jesus Christ.

Reflection Questions

1. Which toxic charities that separate haves and have-nots have you seen and in what ways have you participated in them?
2. In what ways have you kept silent about issues of justice in your faith community? On social media? At

gatherings with friends/family? Politically? What was the cost of your silence?

3. In what ways have you prioritized a narrow view of safety over freedom? How can you move beyond the false binary of safety versus freedom?

4. If you are a white person, in what ways has white supremacy limited your relationships and witness to the gospel? What is at stake for you in Black liberation?

5. Who in your life walks against the "moving walkway" of white supremacy? In what ways do they actively oppose white supremacy and live out antiracism?

Action Items

- Learn about the difference between charity and true mutual aid. You could start here: https://bigdoorbrigade .com/what-is-mutual-aid/.

- Join mutual aid circles or partner with others to help create one in your community.

5

ENDURANCE AS RESISTANCE

I solemnly urge you: proclaim the message; be persistent whether the time is favorable or unfavorable; convince, rebuke, and encourage, with the utmost patience in teaching. . . . Endure suffering, do the work of an evangelist, carry out your ministry fully.

—2 Timothy 4:1b–2, 5b

I normally wear a size-eight shoe. But I bought some clearance size-ten boots in November 2014. I wanted to have room to layer a couple of those really thick, fuzzy socks. It had started getting chilly in Missouri, and the Uprising in Ferguson showed no sign of stopping, despite my prediction early on that it would fizzle out in a few weeks. Gone were my days of pencil skirts and high heels at protests. Now I was layering parka over fleece over hoodie over long-sleeve T-shirt like a puffy marshmallow person. And I was still cold.

During the Uprising, people would bring protesters homemade knit hats and scarves and mittens. Back then we would chant, "We young, we strong, we marchin' alllll night long." But grannies who couldn't march all night long would come by where we were stationed in the Andy Wurm Tire & Wheel lot across from the police department and drop off things to keep us warm. On at least one occasion, I remember someone dropping off a bunch of vitamin C, lecturing us to take our vitamins because we were going to catch a cold standing out there. We took turns bringing hot chocolate or coffee for each other. One time there was a sale at Aldi on glow sticks, so I brought some of those too. When mid-November came, we hung a couple of ornaments on the tree in the parking lot.

Officer Darren Wilson had still not been indicted on any charges for murdering Michael Brown. The state prosecuting attorney at that time was a Democrat named Bob McCulloch, who, after sustained protests and property damage, made a show of presenting the case before a grand jury even though he had no intention of moving forward with charges. Bob McCulloch was a known obstacle to justice in St. Louis County in the eyes of activists. All prosecutors have deep ties to law enforcement because of the ways their jobs intersect, but McCulloch's connection to the police in St. Louis was personal too. His father was a cop who had died in the line of duty. His mother, brother, uncle, and cousin also worked for the St. Louis Police Department. He has gone on record saying that he would've been a police officer himself, except that he had lost his leg to a rare cancer in his late teens.[1] He has a history of refusing to prosecute obvious instances of police violence and brutality.

Activists and Black politicians in Missouri tried to get McCulloch to recuse himself or to get the governor, Jay Nixon (another Democrat), to appoint a special prosecutor. But they wouldn't. Bob McCulloch remained the prosecutor throughout the Ferguson Uprising and only left when activists organized around the Democratic primary in 2018 to say #ByeBob and replaced him with Wesley Bell.

The many ways that Bob McCulloch set the case up to fail would come out later.[2] But in November, all we had was a sense of impending doom and a heavy feeling of dread. Events in the community and in the churches I worked with were constantly being rescheduled, pushed back, or abbreviated because the grand jury could make a decision at any moment, and a public response was inevitable. The entire region was constantly on edge, National Guard at the ready, wondering when the announcement would come.

I had scheduled a conversation in Ferguson with youth from the Episcopal Diocese of Missouri. We planned to do some media training and an analysis of the way the stories had been reported, hear from activists on the ground, volunteer with the Food Pantry at St. Stephen's and the Vine, and then make a pilgrimage to Mike Brown's memorial site on Canfield Drive to pray. St. Louis County is like many counties in the United States; it is very segregated. Youth in the wealthy western suburbs, predominantly white, live a very different reality than the majority Black neighborhoods up north like Ferguson. The hope was to dispel some of the misconceptions about Ferguson and the Uprising in general.

Some white parents complained and asked why we didn't invite the police to be on a panel too. I told them that they can hear the police narrative any time they want by listening to their press conferences and that I was not about to make Black activists sit in a room with the people who had been tear-gassing and beating them.

But there was no way that I could keep that event in November with the threat of the grand jury announcement looming, especially not if I wanted to get some of those white high schoolers from the suburbs to come. Their parents would not have allowed it, and frankly, I also didn't want to be responsible for a room full of teenagers if something did happen. So we rescheduled for January.

On Monday, November 24, I was with my daughter Alice at the doctor's office for a checkup. Alice was seven years old and a charmer. She had nicknames for the doctors and was a favorite of the nurses, and she was growing like a weed. She had missing teeth and the sweetest little voice—her Sierra Leonean accent, which has now faded, was still pretty pronounced at that time. She wiggled next to me on the bench in the waiting room, the tan vinyl squeaking with every move she made, when breaking news came on the television.

The grand jury was going to announce their decision that day.

It was early afternoon at that point, maybe about 1:30 p.m. I called my spouse and said, "It's happening." Adam left the office to accompany Alice to her appointment. I gave them both a kiss goodbye, squeezed Alice with tears in my eyes, and flew out the door to drive to Ferguson with my heart racing.

After all of this waiting, waiting, waiting, we were finally going to get an answer. No one I knew was very hopeful about an indictment. But the waiting ramped up our anxiety all the same. Not knowing what day an announcement would come and what the outcome would be for sure made all of us nervous wrecks. And finally the day was here.

When I got to the Ferguson Police Department, I parked my car a couple of blocks away. Hundreds of people were gathered there, waiting, with more coming. Someone had brought speakers to amplify the announcement when it came so we could all hear it. As the hours went by, over a thousand people arrived. Why would the prosecutor announce that a decision was made and then continue to keep us waiting? People were becoming more and more agitated when the sun began to set. It got even colder, and I was grateful I had bought those size-ten boots and worn layers of fluffy socks.

A tent was set up across from the Ferguson Police Department with warming stations and supplies. In anticipation of the grand jury announcement, we had assembled tear-gas kits: masks, goggles, bottles full of a one-to-one ratio of Maalox and water, and handkerchiefs. We had apple-cider vinegar in case of pepper spray and earplugs for sound cannons and flash-bangs. There were cereal bars and water for weary protesters who had been out for far too long. Some of these tear-gas kits were assembled on the high altar in the nave at Christ Church Cathedral, where I worked and often went at lunch to pray.

When I arrived at the police department, I texted some fellow activists so that we could meet up. We called each other the Ferguson Fam. Tony was there to livestream, and Alicia and I wandered over to the warming tent where I saw another activist, a white middle-aged man named Bob who was also an independent journalist.

"I mean, I know they aren't going to indict him," Bob said, "but what if they did?"

"What if we were preparing for a disaster," I said, "and they actually just . . . indicted him?"

Looking back, this was part naivete due to my whiteness and desire to still have some kind of faith in the system. But it was also the beginning of our grieving process. It was denial. Because we knew that what was going to happen would be so, so bad.

"I should've brought champagne!" Bob said. "I think they'll do it. We should be popping champagne tonight." We laughed and joked about going to get some champagne even though we knew deep down that no one would be celebrating that night.

As the day turned to evening turned to night, we were still waiting. More and more people were coming. The crowd was impatient, bumping up against each other. Sometimes chanting. Sometimes dancing. Sometimes playing loud music, much of it hip-hop from the late '80s and '90s. Classics like NWA's "Fuck tha Police." Koach Baruch Frazier, who goes by KB and who would become a dear friend of mine, was there with his drum. Koach is a Black transgender man who is also Jewish. He has said that between being Jewish, trans, and Black, every day he wakes up and sees in the news that someone wants him dead. When KB played the drums at protests, it felt like the heartbeat of a revolution.

Nearby the speakers and surrounded by the crowd was the "Mike Brown car," a white car painted with phrases like "We the people"; "No justice, no peace"; and "I am Mike Brown."

While we were still waiting, we heard that the mayor of St. Louis, Francis Slay (another Democrat), announced that "violence will not be tolerated" tonight. We laughed and asked if anyone had told the police that.

At 8:15 p.m., well after dark, Bob McCulloch made his announcement.

We had been gathered together in a heightened state of tension for hours by that time.

A strained hush fell over all of us as we listened as the prosecutor said, "The grand jury found no probable cause to charge Darren Wilson . . ."

Tears of frustration and grief prickled at the corner of my eyes.

The sound of wailing from Mike's parents pierced the air.

There was a heavy pause.

Silence.

And then a chant rose up: "I believe that we will win! I believe that we will win! I believe that we will win!" The armored police advanced on us, and the air filled with tear gas. And even as we were running, the streets echoed with the steady sounds of drums—KB, the heartbeat of the revolution—along with our pounding footsteps and our pure, hopeful defiance:

"I believe that we will win!"

I think of that moment often. "I believe that we will win." It reminds me of a line from a beloved hymn: "All of us go down to the dust, yet even at the grave we make our song: Alleluia."[3]

I learned from Ferguson that endurance is a form of resistance.

I used to hate the quote from 2 Timothy at the beginning of this chapter. That part of the verse telling us to endure suffering? It felt like a missive from the white upper midwestern culture I was raised in, quietism that told me to be silent about my pain, that standing up for myself or my loved ones was wrong, that speaking honestly about my experiences was disruptive, that it was better for me to shut up. I thought that "enduring suffering" meant I had to just sit there and take it.

But when I experienced the endurance of the Black activists in Ferguson, I saw these verses in an entirely new way. I read them in light of other biblical stories—like Jacob wrestling with God all night in Genesis or the parable that Jesus tells in the Gospel of Luke about the persistent widow who kept bothering the unjust judge. If we think about endurance through the lens of Jacob's wrestling and the widow's persistence, we definitely do not see a message of a nonconfrontational God who thinks it's better to quietly avoid conflict. In Jacob's story, God pursues Jacob for a night of tug-of-war. In Jesus's parable, the unjust judge is worn down by the widow—the Greek here more literally uses a boxing metaphor and says that the judge is afraid the widow will "beat him black-and-blue" with her persistence.

Enduring suffering, I learned, does not mean a sort of passive acceptance of injustice. Instead, enduring suffering has an emphasis on "endurance." It is a message of hope. It says those among us who have been oppressed are tenacious, whereas those with the most privilege tire out.[4] They are creative, whereas the privileged are rigid. They will outlast us. Their suffering has bred in them grit and determination. Their suffering is fuel for defiance. I am reminded of the church father Tertullian, who said, "The blood of the martyrs is the seed of the Church."[5] Or put another way, the contemporary protest signs that say, "They tried to bury us. They didn't know we were seeds."

"I believe that we will win," led by a Black, trans, Jewish man, was a song of endurance. Of defiance. It reminded me of another song birthed in the face of genocide during the Holocaust in 1939. As a Nazi commander in Lublin cruelly ordered the Jewish people to sing to their own execution, their voices rang out, "*Mir veln zey iberlebn, iberlebn, iberlebn.*"

"We will outlive them."[6]

White Christians, in general, do not have this kind of endurance. It is a gift given to people who often find themselves on the underside of power dynamics.

Just like training at the gym requires discomfort to build up endurance so that an athlete can go harder, faster, stronger, longer, our resilience and emotional-spiritual endurance is built up through suffering. This is not to say suffering itself is good or that God wants us to suffer. Womanist theologians have taught me that suffering in itself is not inherently redemptive or something to pursue or strive for.

It is just to say that white people can be particularly fragile because we don't have this sense of endurance. While Black, trans, Jewish activists chant "I believe that we will win!" through tear gas, white people often can't even handle the emotional discomfort of simply talking about racism. If white people want to build up endurance, we have to lean into the discomfort. This is still a privilege. The discomfort that people of color feel is not optional for them. They do not have a choice to opt out of a racist society. White people have the choice of pretending all of this isn't happening or that it doesn't affect us. And we do that often.

We have a choice, as white people, to avoid the suffering of our siblings because we dislike discomfort. Or we can choose to be in solidarity with oppressed people, including our siblings of color, even and especially when it is uncomfortable, because that is when we will be transformed.

This moment—right after the grand jury announcement that had been purposely stalled all day into the night, right after KB's voice rang out, "I believe that we will win!"—is when I saw that man in a hoodie shoot twice into the air and dart behind the police station. People screamed and ducked and kept running. Then I heard the sound of breaking glass as windows were shattered. My heart sunk as the windows of Cathy's Kitchen were broken too, a Black-owned restaurant that served my daughter pie to occupy her mind when I was first arrested for protesting back in October.

The cops were in the street, which had been decorated for the coming holidays. In their riot gear, they stood under a tinsel light-up sign that hung across the road bearing the message "Seasons Greetings."

I turned to Bob. All talk of popping champagne was gone. I'm sure my eyes were wild when I said, "I have a kid!" I don't know if he even knew what I meant at that moment. I said it again: "I have a kid!"

What I meant was this: between the unrestrained violence from the police and the stampede of people, I was afraid that I might die that night. Many of us were. I was thinking to myself, *I'm a mother.* And even though I was out there fighting for my baby's right to live, she still needed me to come home and tuck her in at night. This fear is something that the Black mamas know all too well. They knew it on this night and for generations before.

The tear gas kept billowing, and I kept hearing loud cracks and pops. Maybe sound cannons? Tear-gas canisters? I had been on the edge of the crowd but was running now too, coughing as some of the tear gas blew back.

I don't remember what happened next. All of a sudden, I was in my car a few blocks away, crying and shaking, texting my mom and spouse, "I'm OK." I drove until it felt like I was far enough away and then pulled into a gas station parking lot, collapsed over the steering wheel, and wept.

Christ Church Cathedral, where my office was located, had been holding vigil that night. They had made a plan in advance during all of that waiting that no matter when the grand jury announcement came, there would be a twenty-four-hour vigil. They made the cathedral a sanctuary and said no one could come in to remove another person—not even the cops. Although there were times where police raided or tear-gassed sympathetic churches and secular but well-known community sanctuary spaces, they left the cathedral alone that night.

The dean and priest at the cathedral were friends of mine, people I trusted. The dean, Mike Kinman, in particular, had been out with me for several actions throughout the Uprising. I texted Mike and the priest, Amy, that I was coming, and they met me at the door. Mike hugged me, and I cried while I said over and over, "It's just so terrible," and Amy murmured soothing things to me, put her arm around my shoulder, and led me back to the office so I could change out of my clothes.

I went back into the nave of the cathedral and sat in a chair by myself and stared blankly ahead. Christ Church Cathedral is a neo-Gothic cathedral built around the time of the Civil War. I loved worshipping there because I felt so small, God felt so big, hymns echoed throughout the space, and the organ was so extravagant. The mystery of God was real for me at the cathedral, and it was both comforting and intoxicating.

At the front of the nave is the altar and behind it white stone reredos with carvings of the saints. In the center is a stunning crucifix. The cathedral was open to the neighborhood during the day, and so sometimes people would come in off the street to play the piano or use the bathroom or get some water. I would sit in the first few rows and just breathe in and out and stare at the giant crucifix.

The night of the grand jury announcement, though, I wasn't meditating. I glared at that white stone Jesus with

European features. I clenched my jaw and turned around in my seat. I couldn't even stand to look at him. In that moment, all I could see was a monument to white supremacy.

Every hour during Christ Church Cathedral's vigil, there was a moment of prayer or reflection or song. At one point, we gathered around the altar, the same altar where tear-gas kits were assembled only days earlier, and we prayed.

And as we gathered around the altar, I noticed a young couple with an infant in a carrier. I thought of the screams and clouds of tear gas from earlier that night, and I burst into tears as we prayed, thinking, *The world is ending. Worlds are ending and beginning all the time. And babies are still being born.*

It was only a month away from Christmas, where we celebrate the hope brought to us in a tiny baby Jesus. For me that night, that baby was a sign that God with us. Even though things were as bleak as I had ever seen, justice felt far away, and we were all worn down and brokenhearted after going up against empire and losing, despite all of it, that baby reminded me that *life is stubborn* and *tenacious*, and *new life finds a way.*

The stories in the Hebrew Bible and in the New Testament tell us something about the way that God works and who God is. God brings forth *life* in pure resistance to empires that wage death. And the way that God brings forth these hope-children says something too. God didn't have to come to Earth as an infant; if God was determined to be a human, They could've just appeared as Jesus as an adult. But children are *so special* to God that God just wouldn't feel right unless God came as a child. And not just any child in any family with any birth story. The story of the holy family is not one of the stereotypical nuclear family, with a mom, a dad, 2.5 kiddos, and a dog. God chose, on purpose, that Jesus would be born into a queer family, a polycule of love made up of three parents: a man like Joseph, and a woman like Mary, and a nonbinary Spirit lending Their Holy DNA. God could have pulled this one off all on Their own if They really wanted. This is the God who said "Let there be light" and there was light and by whose Word separated the sea and the dry land. God could've said, "Let there be Me on Earth, enfleshed!" and it would've been done, insta-Jesus appearing on Earth, no problem. God could've done this without Mary's womb and courage and without Joseph faithfully agreeing to this very strange plan. And yet it says something about who God is that God *chooses* to collaborate with humans, to give us the opportunity and the vital role of cocreating alongside God, even in the miracle of the incarnation.

The tiny baby that night in the cathedral was a sign to me of God's presence. When it felt like the world had ended and we had lost all hope, when we were angry and hurting and afraid, God was with us. Even in destruction, God is here, birthing this new world that is coming.

God continued to give signs of God's presence during those times. When I left the cathedral, I went to the Episcopal Church of the Holy Communion, where my friend Rebecca was the priest, and I slept on the floor with a few other people, ready to get up and protest when the morning came a few hours later.

We woke up and bundled up and headed out in the streets in the cold to protest, blocking the freeway. We put on masks as the police began to pepper spray nonviolent demonstrators and tried to be there to bear witness to what was happening. As we ran from the police, an older woman was having trouble keeping up. Rebecca grabbed her and said, "Are you OK?" and brought her along with us until we were all safe.

When it was time to head home, I checked my phone. I saw the text alert that said more than 175 cities had held protests that day. I was so tired and so overwhelmed, I started crying again.

I wasn't like KB. I wasn't a Black freedom fighter. I wasn't full of his faith. I wasn't sure that we would win.

But if we were going down swinging, at least we weren't alone.

There are signs of God's Spirit at work all around us. Messages of solidarity. Reminders of God's promises. Moments inviting us into challenges. For those of us within the white church, we can think of building up endurance for discomfort during antiracist work as a spiritual discipline in the same way we think of reading Scripture or prayer. We should be disciplined in seeking out the very things that make us uncomfortable because those are the moments in which we can be transformed. God gives us these opportunities. They are all around us. It is on us to say yes to them and then to lean into the experience instead of burning out, freezing up, or getting defensive.

Our siblings of color and other oppressed people have had no choice but to build up this endurance. In our society, even and especially in denominations like the ELCA, people of color suffer endless violence. Sometimes this takes the form of microaggressions, but other times, it is pure overt racism. Many people of color in our church have courageously expressed exhaustion from having to endure white people who refuse to do our own work on antiracism.

Not all people of color protest in the streets. Many do racial justice work in other ways. But some don't, for their own reasons. White people need to remember that people of color don't owe us anything. Their very survival is a protest. Their normal lives are full of resistance.

Black activists are some of the strongest people I know. But they shouldn't have to be this strong. Black women in particular have told us that stereotypes like the "strong Black woman" are killing them, and the expectation to be able to endure any hardship makes their bones and spirit tired. Blue Telusma has said that the stereotype of the strong Black woman has become "a toxic normalized expectation, that's compromised our health; with many in the medical profession now admitting (and proving through extensive studies) that doctors often assume Black women can endure more pain than other women, and therefore need less compassionate care."[7] Black people need to be able to exist without being in a constant state of survival. They deserve lives that are free and full of abundance and rest and care.

It is our job as white people to do the work we have been neglecting for so long so that can be a reality.

Reflection Questions

1. What messages did you learn in church or at home about suffering?
2. When is it difficult to have hope?
3. Is there a time you experienced a sign of God's presence?
4. What areas in your life is God calling you to build endurance?
5. How is God calling you to cocreate alongside Them[8] in this movement?
6. Has your congregation or local faith community served as a refuge during societal unrest? If yes, how? If no, why not?

Action Items

- Commit to doing something Desiree Lynn Adaway suggests: reading only Black voices for a period of time and amplifying these beacons of hope and resilience on your social media.
- If you are physically able, show up at a protest that is out of your comfort zone (and continue to do so). These might be protests held at night, protests without permits, or riskier actions like highway shutdowns and so on. Notice who is there and who isn't and how it affects the way the police treat the crowd.

6

COMMUNITY CARE
AS RESISTANCE

The greatness of a community is most accurately measured by the
compassionate actions of its members.

—Coretta Scott King[1]

In the Midwest where I grew up, the concept of the so-called
protestant work ethic had a tight grip on the culture—the
idea, sometimes explicit and sometimes just beneath the surface, that a person's willingness to work hard was a reflection of their moral character. I learned early on that nonstop
work was something to be admired. People talked about
themselves as "workaholics," but they meant it in a good
way, as a humblebrag. It was a way of saying, "I am a good person. I earn my keep."

A feature of white supremacy and racialized capitalism is valuing people solely based on what they produce. Think, for example, of the way that we commodify basic needs. The fact that health insurance is tied to employment for nearly all people in the United States means that if you are unemployed, you are unlikely to get the health care that you need. All of our basic needs, like water, food, or shelter, have been commodified, meaning they all cost money. So in order to be able to survive, you have to work. And with the rising cost of living and stagnant wages in much of the country, many people are working several jobs, existing paycheck to paycheck, and drowning in debt.

As a survivor of abuse, I spent a lot of time listening to a demonic track play in my head about my own self-worth. It told me that what happened to me was my fault, that I was bad, dirty, or wrong. It told me that I was disposable. One way that I tried to deal with this painful internal narrative was to make sure that I was worthy. If I was perfect and hardworking, maybe then I would be deserving. Maybe then I would safe.

In high school, I enlisted in every club I could, every extracurricular, every volunteer activity. And I sought after excellence in my grades. Math didn't come naturally to me, and so I would stay after class every day before cheerleading practice to get more tutoring with my teacher. I worked on my homework in front of her so that she could correct me every step of the way. I obsessed about my grades, studying for hours and hours to maintain a 4.0 GPA.

As I have learned more about antiracism and features of white culture, I discovered that perfectionism is a reflection of whiteness. It is one of the calling cards of white culture. If white supremacy and racialized capitalism put people in the precarious position of conditional safety, we learn that not being good enough means that we are disposable. Making a mistake or failing or not measuring up means we are expendable. So both inside of racial justice work and in our regular lives, people like me, who have internalized this narrative, overwork to prove our worth, to prove that we are good enough.

Looking back, I can see now that some of the biggest mistakes I have made in racial justice work or community organizing happened because I failed to slow down. My judgment was impaired because I was overfunctioning. I was unable to notice my own red flags and warning signs because I didn't pause long enough to reflect.

During most of the first year of the Ferguson Uprising, I was going to therapy once a month. During one session with my therapist, she begged me to consider stepping back a little in order to get my post-traumatic stress disorder (PTSD) under control. I told her I would. And then the next time we met, she opened up our session by saying, "So I saw a picture of you protesting on the *New York Times* news website this week."

Busted.

So when people ask me for advice about liberation work—like when new activists began reaching out to me during the renewed wave of protests in 2020—I tell them that they need to make sure they take care of themselves *and each other*. I had more privilege than pretty much everyone else during the Ferguson Uprising, and I am still deeply affected by the things I saw and experienced.

Perhaps I was so deeply affected because, as a white person, I had a lot less endurance built up around racial discomfort—something I've mentioned before. Much of the exhaustion I felt was because of my own need to catch up. I needed to be stretched in order to build up capacity, to strengthen my muscles so that I could develop the stamina necessary for this work. During the protests following the murder of George Floyd in 2020, I saw other white people express similar experiences. A few weeks of protests, a few weeks of conflict with racist family members or strain in our workplaces, and we were all totally exhausted.

There is a tension here. Antiracist work is always full of tension, but elements of white participation in that work are especially fraught. We run the risk of making one of two common mistakes, which at first seem at odds with one another.

White people often rush into action with a messy urgency that does more harm than good. Action is a good thing. But it is also important for those of us who are white to examine our motives, particularly when we are new to antiracist work. Sometimes action is a way to avoid dealing with our discomfort. As in "I feel white guilt, so I am going to try to alleviate this awful feeling by proving to myself I am a good person. If I go to enough protests and just earn enough proverbial antiracism scout badges, then everyone will know I am a good person." This franticness is a way of distancing ourselves from the ways we are implicated in these systems. By focusing on proving our own sense of goodness or worthiness, we are continuing to center whiteness.

On the flip side, another pitfall that white people fall into is a failure to take any real action. We avoid anything that calls for risk or sacrifice. We instead intellectualize everything—signing up for book clubs or participating in an endless introspection that results in no tangible changes to our communities. We put everything up for committee and discuss it endlessly in disembodied debates. We do all this because for many white people, racism feels abstract. We don't experience the physical, emotional, and psychological effects of racism. Learning is good, it is important, but we can get caught up in our heads doing a ton of journaling and book reading and "dialogue" while people are literally dying in the streets.

Liberation requires *both* external work and internal work.

For myself, I have found that an intentional "action–reflection–action" cycle is important. When I participate with others in tangible and external antiracist actions, real things change in my community. And when I take the time to reflect on how I showed up to that work, how I felt about it, what I think God is calling to me next, that internal work has the potential to transform me as an individual too. When I take action, I get to meet people in my community doing this work, and when I reflect, I can discern how to get connected with the generations-long struggle for liberation in a way that makes sense for the needs of the movement as well as my own gifts and spheres of influence.

This work is indeed exhausting for white people *because of our own fragility*. And yet as Ella's song reminds us, "We who believe in freedom cannot rest until it comes." Any exhaustion that white people face doing antiracism work is nothing compared to the never-ending, soul-sucking experience of being a person of color constantly subjected to a racist society. For the past several hundred years, although white people have been the cause of racial suffering, we have not borne our part of the responsibility to end it. That has left Black and Brown people and other people of color doing work that isn't theirs just to survive.

This idea of self-care and rest is complicated. On the one hand, white people need to build up the endurance to do this work for the long haul. But on the other hand, we do not need a bunch of white people who are not at our best showing up and making reactive, unsafe decisions that are harmful and put people of color at risk because we haven't done the work of caring for ourselves. Rest and self-care are essential. And we have to also provide opportunities for community care to ensure that people of color can also rest. We cannot go to a few protests and peter out while our siblings are still dying in the streets.

In Ferguson, there were regular spaces curated for Black activists only. These spaces were important because they were places to be able to speak freely without having to cater to white feelings or white guilt. Black women often organized healing circles and gathered resources for things like massages or spiritual care. The daily danger of being Black coupled with the ongoing physical violence and terrorism by the police during protests meant that Black activists were suffering in body and in mind.

One of my comrades, Alexis Templeton, a Black nonbinary person in the movement, pointed out to me that systems like white supremacy are counting on activists burning out. They said that for Black people, just waking up every day was a radical act of resistance in a society that wants you dead.

Ferguson taught me that for marginalized people especially, rest is not a break from the revolution; rest is revolutionary.

After I left Missouri and began organizing in other cities or in other spaces, particularly with organizations founded or led primarily by white people, I noticed a huge change in the way things operated. In Ferguson, although it was no utopia and there was plenty of division within the activist circles, there was a sense of nurturing and community that was lacking in white-led organizing spaces because of an internalized false sense of individualism that is a part of white culture.

When I tried to articulate this I was told that the things I missed, like community meals, were "not strategic" or a good use of our resources. I fundamentally disagree with that assessment precisely because of my time in Ferguson. I believe that organizing "wins" are important, and strategy matters. But treating activists like cogs in a machine that exist only to achieve a certain purpose is mimicking the values of white supremacy and racialized capitalism. It is almost the very definition of what Audre Lorde called the "master's tools" when she wrote, "For the master's tools will never dismantle the master's house. They may allow us temporarily to beat him at his own game, but they will never enable us to bring about genuine change."[2] White people are the "masters" here. And even when we try to escape that role to be a part of liberation work, even when we wish to be antiracist, we are often still picking up the same old tools, such as the cultural norms valuing individualism and dictating that productivity is the basis of human worth.

Those of us working for justice *must* carve out moments of liberation *now* so that we can remember what we are fighting for. Moments of rest and community care and mutual aid are glimpses of the future we are building. I caught sight of this future again when I started organizing with SOUL in Chicago. The executive director, Tanya Watkins, is a Black woman who prioritizes community care and organizing rooted in love.

Part of the strength, I think, of the leadership in St. Louis and Ferguson was the way it centered Black women. It was Black women who brought both ferocity and tenderness to the organizing happening there, and everyone who came into contact with their work was changed. In the fall of 2014, a group of people arranged to get the Black women who were leading chants and marches pedicures. To me this was reminiscent of the Maundy Thursday ritual during Holy Week when we remember Jesus's command to love one another by washing each other's feet. This gift of gratitude was both symbolic and practical because, as you can imagine, marching for days on end is hard on your feet.

I have many memories of the ways that community care happened both on and off the streets in Ferguson and St. Louis during the Uprising. People were diligent in creating moments of those "glimpses" where we could see the just world we are seeking shining through despite all of the setbacks and disappointments. I was especially moved by the ways that Black women of all ages welcomed my daughter Alice. Pastor Traci Blackmon would reference Alice and other baby activists and remind us, through an adaptation of the Assata chant, that "it is our duty to fight for *their* freedom." When I spoke to other parents of Black children—mothers, in particular—this was the motivating factor that kept us all going. When people asked me why I was so invested in the Ferguson Uprising, I told them, "I don't want to leave this for my children to deal with."

We wanted a world where our babies could be free.

A group of those of us who were mothers of children about the same age began to get them together. We would gather together at actions like marches or meetings, but we would also meet up for playdates or birthday parties. Nurse and activist Brittany Ferrell approached me once at an event I had coordinated where she was a panelist and asked if our children could get together sometime. She said that she wanted to be intentional about showing her daughter, Kenna, that families were made up in all kinds of ways, and of course our family was created via transracial adoption. I was so floored and inspired by her diligence in parenting.

As a white mother of Black children, I am constantly thinking about making sure that my daughters have racial mirrors and representation in their media, in our relationships, and in our community. My children don't have the privilege of looking at their parents' faces and seeing their own faces reflected back, and so providing those opportunities is so important. I was grateful to have my daughter spend social time with revolutionary people like Brittany and Kenna.

Alice was invited to Kenna's birthday party that year, which was at a rock-climbing gym. Alice's party for her ninth birthday was a Hollywood-themed affair. I cherish a powerful, beautiful photograph from that event of Alice, Kenna, and another activist baby wearing their fanciest outfits, donning sunglasses, and raising a Black Power fist on a red carpet mock-up at our house.

It is our duty to fight for their *freedom.*

These moments might seem somehow outside of the revolution, but they were revolutionary, because the revolution was motivated by wanting our children to have the carefree childhood they deserved.

A carefree childhood is something so often stolen from Black children. White people like to think that children are immune to racism, but the data doesn't bear that out. Studies say that children recognize race as babies and develop racial biases between the ages of three to five.[3] Many of the Black people in my life tell me that their first memories of racism start in early elementary school. That was Alice's experience. In the school that she attended in Missouri, during her first-grade art class, a little white boy leaned over to tell Alice that "Black people are not beautiful." She cried.

The advice of adult transracial adoptees told me that having positive representation and instilling cultural pride was particularly important for Black children with white parents. So after debriefing with Alice at home about what happened, we decided together on the next steps, and the following day she wore a shirt featuring several civil rights heroes. Dr. Danielle J. Buhuro teaches in her book *Spiritual Care in the Age of #BlackLivesMatter* that cultural pride is an important part of spiritual care for Black people.[4] That civil rights T-shirt fortified Alice; she was wearing the armor of Black pride as she went back to school the next day.

But Black children should not need armor.

My children have different rules than the ones I had growing up as a white child. They can't play with toy guns. Tamir Rice was only twelve years old when the police in Cleveland rolled up and shot and killed him. The police fired their guns before their vehicle had even come to a complete stop. And when Tamir's sister ran to his aid, they cuffed her and put her in the back of the police vehicle. Because of this story, my kids don't even play with squirt guns.

The horror of Tamir's story was my final push away from criminal justice reformism. I used to think if we increased police departments' budgets with more body cameras, more antibias training, that things would get better. I started to notice, though, that this was more than the individual actions of a minority of officers. If not all police were bad, why did they consistently elect openly racist white nationalists to represent them as the heads of their unions? In St. Louis, the police union is so racist that the Black cops have their own union. Why were police with multiple excessive force complaints the ones who were often promoted and given higher positions of authority? It is important to ask, "Who do cops say are the good cops?" And when we look at the answer to that, we see that people who are promoted, people who are elected to high positions, like the representative of the Fraternal Order of Police, are almost always people who have *high* levels of excessive force complaints and a record of explicit white supremacy. This is consistent across many departments and across states. Police are telling us who they are and what they think based on who they elect to represent them. And it is almost always people who are infamously racist like Bob Kroll in Minneapolis, Jeffrey Roorda in St. Louis, or John Catanzara in Chicago.

Once Tamir was killed, I gave up on the idea that this was just "a few bad apples" and started believing Black activists when they told me the entire tree was rotten, from the roots up. As John the Baptist warned the religious aristocracy in Matthew 3:10, "Even now the ax is lying at the root of the trees; every tree therefore that does not bear good fruit is cut down and thrown into the fire." I saw the way the police treated Tamir and his sister, and I thought, *There is nothing in this system worth saving. It has to be destroyed so we can build something new.*

That is when I began to believe in police and prison abolition. I didn't believe in it all at once. It was so radically different than the things I had grown up believing. But I started questioning the idea that the same police who shot a child with a toy actually made us safer. I started listening to activists and theorists and experts about what *does* make us safer, like access to medical care, education, housing, therapy, healthy food, rest, joy, and other basic human rights. Little by little, the vision that abolitionists were casting made more and more sense.

Now that my daughters are teenagers, the stakes feel even higher, and as they progress developmentally, it is even harder to carve out space for them to have the carefree moments they deserve. Trayvon Martin was only a teenager when he went to the store to get some Skittles and tea and was killed by vigilante George Zimmerman. Because of this story, my teens don't wear their hoodies up.

When the stories of Ahmaud Arbery, Breonna Taylor, George Floyd, Tony McDade, and so many other victims of anti-Blackness and violence unraveled in the media throughout 2020, a feeling of heaviness took over my house. As teenagers discerning their own identity and place in the world, things hit my daughters much differently than when they were younger. As news of police violence went international, our friends and family in Sierra Leone reached out to me to ask if the girls were safe. It felt like a punch in the gut to know that there are no guarantees. I had made promises to two countries, to families, to loved ones to take care of these girls. I feel accountable to their ancestors to keep them safe and give them lives full of joy. But even when Black kids and teens do all the "right things," sometimes they don't make it home.

Attending protests in 2020 was cathartic for them. It was a place they could chant or hold signs and express the pain and anger they felt at the ways their moments of rest and opportunities for a carefree childhood had been stolen from them. And perhaps even more important, they got to see in Chicago the thousands and thousands of people coming out for months on end to fight for their freedom, for their right to carefree teenage moments. Those protests helped them know they weren't alone, that there were people who cared. If you were in the streets in your town or city during that time, thank you. The news of widespread and sustained protests did a lot to boost the morale in my household.

When police escalated their violence during protests in Chicago, I took a day to discern what my role might be in this moment. I knew that if there were instances of property damage, the police would respond violently, and I was afraid of what my children would hear from our apartment. After the initial protest we attended as a family, we made the decision to send my daughters to be with my sister and her family for the week so that they wouldn't hear the police violence in our neighborhood, and Adam and I could spend the week in the streets. We texted their teacher, another Black woman, and told her that they were "calling in Black" to school the next day. She affirmed that decision. I told them their only job that week was to focus on joy, comfort, and connection. Any carefree, restful moments they could grab on to for themselves were revolutionary moments.

After picking them up at the end of their week of fun, we planned to do some of their favorite things like making homemade sushi or playing card games. I took the next week off work, and even though we continued to attend protests and actions, I turned off my email and paused other conversations to focus on making sure they were able to breathe.

That grind culture of capitalism is so internalized in me that even in liberation work, it is surprisingly easy to get so wrapped up in activism and neglect real flesh-and-blood people right in front of me. I have to pause sometimes so that I can love my family well and remember why we are in this struggle, because as one of our friends in Sierra Leone said to me, "Their Black lives matter too."

If you are a white person, maybe antiracism or activism is new for you. Even for those people who have been doing this for a long time, the new challenges we are facing, such as the ongoing pandemic, make this work new again for us too. We have been forced to figure out how to care for one another and make change in our communities in ways that are different from what we are used to. Maybe you, like me, feel a frantic itch inside you to do something. All of us need to pause and reflect, not to walk away from the work but to work from a place of health. We must take action, but that action should not be out of our own reactivity or for our own selfish motives in order to assuage our own guilt.

Jesus challenges us to be ready to give up our very lives for the sake of our neighbor. And he also promises us, "Come to me, all you that are weary and are carrying heavy burdens, and I will give you rest."[5] Jesus tells us that these things are not at odds with one another but work together. He models both sacrifice *and* self-care and community care for us. He takes time away alone. He spends time with his closest friends. Jesus knows that for marginalized people, rest is not a break from the revolution; rest is revolutionary.

As a community organizer, I sometimes lead groups in an activity where I ask them to write on sticky notes what they think liberation is. They are invited to think of a moment where they got one of those glimpses of liberation and to describe it or to use their imagination to dream one up. When we reach liberation for all people, how will we know? What will it smell like, taste like, look like, sound like, and feel like? In all of the times I have led or participated in that activity, no one has ever said that liberation looks like constant laboring. They describe eating their grandma's pie or dance parties on the roof with their friends or the smell of a newborn baby. These are moments of rest and leisure and community care. And they are sacred.

Genesis tells us that God created the world in six days, bit by bit, part by part. And on the seventh day, God rested. I like to think that on that day, God *created* rest and established it as one of Her most hallowed creations. We will know we have reached liberation when there is rest, both in body and in spirit. For all people.

Reflection Questions

1. What messages have you heard glorifying productivity over rest?
2. What red flags or warning signs do you see in yourself that signal that it is time to recalibrate and find balance? How can white people honor our need for rest without prioritizing ourselves over the needs of marginalized people?
3. What glimpses of liberation have you seen or experienced already?
4. Name a moment when the community came together to care for you. What was that like?
5. How can you provide community care so that Black activists can get the rest they need and deserve?[6]

Action Items

- Find a Black-led or other people of color–led community care collective and raise money in support. Contribute to the spiritual, mental, emotional, and physical care of Black people, especially Black activists. If you don't know of a collective in your community, you can raise money for Jamaa Birth Village in Ferguson, which has Brittany Ferrell (a Black activist from St. Louis) on their board and focuses on caring for Black mothers and babies: https://jamaabirthvillage.org/.

- Find out more about the ways that reparation funds are organized in your community. Commit to contributing to organizations and individuals. For example, you might anonymously send money each month to a Black trans woman or commit to organizing the white parents at your child's preschool to fund 50 percent of the tuition for Black and Indigenous students.

7

JOY AS RESISTANCE

In a society that wants to steal your joy, every smile is an act of resistance.

—Alexis Templeton[1]

If you remember, in August 2014, I thought all of the strife of the Ferguson Uprising was going to blow over. When I heard about a weekend of mass resistance in October, I was skeptical. I figured the momentum would be lost by then. I was wrong. Thousands of people had come to St. Louis for Ferguson October.

Just a few days before the weekend began, St. Louis police officer Jason Flanery killed Black teen Vonderrit Myers Jr., a.k.a. Droop. Flanery was off duty and working another job doing private security. In other words, Flanery had been working more than one job and was undoubtedly exhausted, which many of us believe impaired his judgment. The police said that Droop had a gun, but in a video of him buying a sandwich at a gas station minutes earlier, he didn't appear to be armed. His family insisted there was no gun.

By this point, I had seen the way that police blatantly lie in these instances and had heard stories from Black people in St. Louis about the ways police plant guns. Only a few months before Michael Brown was murdered, another young Black man in St. Louis, Terry Robinson, secretly recorded St. Louis police officers handcuffing and detaining him.[2] In the video, the police pressure Robinson to give them names of people whom they hoped to frame by planting guns. Only a few months later, we would all see video play out on the national stage when Michael Slager planted a stun gun on Walter Scott after shooting him in the back to justify murdering him. Just last winter, a Baltimore police officer was federally charged with planting evidence: a BB gun on someone in 2014 and drugs on someone else in 2015.[3] Over and over, on the news and in person, I have seen cops lie to justify their crimes. So I believed Droop's family when they said he was unarmed.

Jason Flanery was never charged with Droop's murder. But a couple years later, he was fired from the police unit and charged with a DWI when he crashed a police vehicle on the job while drunk and high on cocaine.[4] Flanery was not tested for drugs or alcohol the day he killed Droop.

Droop's death just before Ferguson October heightened the tension even more. Droop had been killed on the south side of St. Louis in the Shaw neighborhood, and Michael Brown had been killed in a northern suburb. Now the protests were spread all over St. Louis County.

The weekend of Ferguson October was full of actions, marches, meetings, and workshops. On October 12, I attended what was called a "mass meeting," which included speakers and an interfaith prayer service. It was held on the Saint Louis University (SLU) campus in Chaifetz Arena, and there were well over a thousand people in attendance, including some prominent activists and academics like Dr. Cornel West and famous Christian authors like Jim Wallis. The event began with a lineup of clergy from various traditions. The speakers were nearly all Black people, but they were professional folks and leaders in formal organizations, as opposed to those in the crowd—raw, young Black activists who had been out on the street nonstop for over sixty days. At a certain point, the crowd began to murmur.

Someone yelled, "This is bullshit!" and the crowd began chanting, "Let them speak!" That is how the mass meeting got taken over by the young people most affected by everything that had happened. They were unwilling to sit through pageantry or speakers they felt were out of touch. Pastor Traci Blackmon, who had been moderating the event, shifted the lineup and introduced the activists: "The next voice we hear will be a word from the streets." Tef Poe and other millennial activists urged clergy to be present in the streets, to take real action instead of posturing at meetings, and to take direction from the people who had already been in the streets for a while.

After the mass meeting takeover, the local activists began marching. We met up at various places and left in shifts. I had no idea where we were going; I just followed the crowd.

We walked silently on the sidewalk. But even though we weren't even in the street at this point, the police showed up, highly militarized. In riot gear, they tapped their batons on the ground in unison. It was an intimidation tactic, and it worked. My heart accelerated, wondering what they would do. It's hard to describe the visceral response that bodies have to these kinds of nonverbal threats and fear tactics, especially after two months of being terrorized by militarized police. The rhythmic banging of their batons was haunting. It felt like they were conjuring up an evil force.

We reached our destination—the center of the SLU campus. When security tried to stop us from coming on campus, an SLU student held her student ID card up and said, "These are my guests." Thus began Occupy SLU. I stayed for the teach-in that first night and throughout the week visited to drop off supplies. For six days, protesters occupied the SLU campus at the clock tower, hosting daily teach-ins. Eventually, SLU acquiesced to some of the activists' demands in an agreement that came to be known as the Clock Tower Accords. The accords had thirteen agreements, including an increased budget for the African American studies program, increased aid to support the retention of Black students at SLU, and others. While the protests were about Mike and Droop, focused on state violence and police brutality, these young Black activists knew that entire systems were implicated in the death of Black people, including the slow death of the denial of resources in areas like education or health care. These pieces are connected, and so their solutions must take a systemic approach. The conversations around abolition and defunding the police make these connections by reallocating funds from death-dealing police forces into life-giving community resources.

On Monday, October 13, 2014, the weekend culminated with an interfaith direct action against the Ferguson Police Department. There were hundreds of us, of various ages and races and genders, both clergy and lay, occupying the Ferguson PD's parking lot, praying, singing, and chanting with our hands up. All of this in the midst of a complete downpour, a thunderstorm, but we had decided that we would stay in the parking lot for at least four and a half hours—the same amount of time that Mike Brown's body lay in the street on Canfield Drive in the baking August sun.

The police lined up, shoulder to shoulder, two rows deep in front of us, carrying riot shields and batons. My friend's little brother, Matthew, was in town. He was nineteen and Black. I was only twenty-six at the time, but I felt responsible for him because of my friendship with his sister. He pushed to the front of the riot line, and so I followed him until I was face-to-face with the police (although it feels strange to call it face-to-face with how much equipment was between us). The police kept pushing us back with their riot shields until, between the people behind me and the police in front of me, I lost any sense of balance and could no longer stand up. The demonstrators behind us were physically holding up our weight.

I didn't realize I had started crying until an older Black woman reached over and used her thumb to wipe underneath my eye where the mascara had been running—not only because of my tears but because of the sheets of rain that continued to pound down on us.

This was one of the times when I smelled what I thought might be alcohol on a cop's breath. I noticed his leg was bouncing nervously. I looked into his eyes. He looked so young.

The police got quiet and still for a second.

Then I saw a shield come right at me, and the next thing I knew, my knee was throbbing with pain, my wrist hurt, and I was on my knees on the ground.

I don't actually remember a lot of what happened next; I blocked it out except for a few snapshots. What I do know I only know because people have shown me photos and videos or told me about it.

At a certain point, the first line of police rotated out, and the second line forced their way in. An officer started beating me with his club. I put my head down on my knees and covered it with my arms, and the officer continued to hit my back and neck. I do remember trying to calm myself down by repeating to myself that if I got hit in the face, it would be OK. It would be OK.

I heard an older Black man behind me yell something at the officer along the lines of "Pick on someone your own size," and the baton stopped hitting me. I looked up to make sure Matthew was OK. An officer was holding a baton against his throat with such force that he knocked his glasses off and he was choking. I scrambled for Matthew's glasses as I said as loudly and calmly as I could to the officer next to him, "Stop him! He can't breathe! Look! Stop!" trying to make eye contact with him, and then turned to Matthew and said, "I'm right here, Matthew. It's going to be OK. Don't touch him." I was so afraid of what they would do to Matthew if he pushed the officer's hands away.

The police moved back, regrouped, and created another formation while Matthew and I moved back from the riot line.

Eventually, the police started arresting people. I was arrested by a middle-aged highway patrol officer who put the handcuffs tight around my wrists. I watched officers body-slam a Black pastor with long locks to the ground as one of them screamed, "Stop resisting!" They led us into the precinct garage to fill out paperwork, but it took forever because the pens and papers were soaked from the rain and wouldn't work. There were so many municipalities and departments there, the police were arguing about how to fill out the paperwork. The person writing on the slip of paper said, "I am just charging them all with disturbing the peace, resisting arrest, and assaulting an officer." The highway patrol officer who arrested me said, "She didn't touch me. Just put disturbing the peace." I later learned that the Black pastor who the police had violently slammed to the ground was charged with resisting arrest and the assault of an officer.

As the police fuddled with pens that wouldn't write, a few of us started singing "Siyahamba," our three-part harmony echoing off the concrete in the garage of the police station: "We are marching in the light of God. / We are marching in the light of God."

I asked multiple times during the initial processing if I could go to the bathroom. Each time, the officers pushed me off, saying, "Maybe later." Then they placed several of us in the back of a police truck, and I remember feeling intense pain because I had to pee so bad. The other arrestees urged me to just pee in the back of the vehicle; they said that they didn't care and that it would be fine. I very seriously considered it, but I was unsure how long I would be held in jail, and I didn't want to be stuck in pee-soaked clothes for days. My clothes were already soaked and damp from the rain; they were uncomfortable enough as is.

The police truck drove around for what seemed like forever. My hands started to go numb from the cuffs. No one would tell us where we were going. No one would answer when I might be able to use a bathroom.

We finally stopped at our first location. We waited on cold, metal chairs until we were called back, one by one. Once I was called up, an officer gruffly told me to face the wall while a female officer slid her hands up between my thighs, around my groin, and then under my bra. I took a sharp breath in, and tears sprung to my face. I wanted to tell her I was a sexual assault survivor, but she was looking at me with obvious disdain, which told me that she probably wouldn't care. I tried to just keep breathing and wait for it to be over.

We had been able to keep our belongings up until this point, something that is not typical in regular arrests, but because of the mass arrests that had taken place, the system was overloaded, and they didn't want to deal with trying to return our belongings to us. As mentioned earlier, this was how I was able to do some clever contortion and get to my phone to live-tweet my arrest and do an interview with the *LA Times* in the back of the police vehicle.

When the reporter who interviewed me ended our conversation by tweeting back the common phrase we used as a greeting in the streets—"Stay safe"—I responded, "God doesn't always call us to safety. God calls us to faithfulness."

The reporter included that final tweet in his piece, but I didn't tweet that to sound heroic. I was contemplating peeing myself in the back of a vehicle in front of relative strangers; this was not a glamorous moment. I tweeted it because I had to remind *myself*. So often the white church has chosen what we call "safety" for ourselves over faithfulness. Too often we choose safety or comfort over the liberation of our siblings. Anytime people from my hometown heard that I was participating in the Uprising in Ferguson, they would clutch their pearls about my safety. But I remembered what Ruby Sales had said to me, what the young Black activists in the streets were modeling for all of us. And I knew that until we kill white supremacy, there will be no "safety" for my family.

I finished the Twitter interview as quickly as I could because I didn't know if they would confiscate my belongings. When we finally arrived at the next location, they made me remove my wedding and engagement ring and hand over my small knapsack with my work cell phone inside as well as my wallet and a homemade tear-gas treatment kit.

At this point, it had been nearly four hours, and I still hadn't been able to go to the bathroom despite asking every person that I had encountered. I finally begged the officer who had me sign the paperwork, and he took pity on me. I only had to wait a few minutes longer for two female officers to take me to the bathroom.

They uncuffed me right before I went into the stall. I was told I could shut the door most of the way but not to lock it, and they stood right there keeping watch and listening to me use the bathroom. After I got out of the stall, I caught a glimpse of my reflection in the mirror. I had thick streams of mascara running down both of my cheeks all the way to my jaw. I asked permission to wash my face, and they shrugged. It seemed like a silly thing to ask, but throughout this whole process, I hadn't been in control of my own body, and so I wasn't sure they would allow me. After I finished, they put the handcuffs back on me.

I started to worry that Adam and Alice would not know where I was. I wasn't even sure where I was. They kept taking us through different hallways and rooms, but the groups of people I was with kept changing. I hadn't seen the people who rode in with me in the police van, and I still hadn't been able to make a phone call.

They lined a bunch of us up against a stone wall and walked us to a back door. There was another police vehicle waiting. We were taken to the so-called justice center for processing and to be put into cells. The cell was cold. I was still damp from the rain and couldn't stop shivering. There was a heavy door with a small window and a hard bench. I was taken to see a nurse who asked questions about my health. I was pressured to just say that everything was fine even though my hands were still numb from the too-tight cuffs and my knee was throbbing. At every step, if we questioned what was happening to us at all, the police would threaten to keep us locked up longer, even overnight.

And so I didn't tell the nurse about my injuries, even though I could see that blood was soaking through my black leggings.

I was eventually ushered into a room with several phones in booths with metal dividers. I called the jail support number for protesters that I had memorized.

The police led me into another room and took our mug shots. At one point, I misunderstood directions about where to stand, and when I asked for clarification, a police officer barked at me to shut up. They gave us brown bags for dinner. I was grateful because I hadn't eaten since before the action, about 9:00 that morning, and it was now evening. I opened the brown bag. It was a piece of bologna between two slices of white bread.

They had us line up in another hallway, and again, I was with people who I didn't know. They kept separating us and moving us around, never telling us where we were going. When I got to the front of the line, I was surprised when a plastic bag of my belongings was shoved in my hand. I turned to the young Black policeman who held open the door for me to leave. I looked him in the eyes and said, "I am praying for you." He held my gaze, swallowed hard, and promised to pray for me too.

When I was released, Adam and Alice had food waiting for me. We went home, and I tried to sleep, but I was filled with anxiety. When I began protesting in Ferguson, I knew I would see things that would be upsetting, but I under-estimated how much it would affect me. Police violence, arrest, jails—they are all traumatic. It was especially trigger-ing for me to experience such a lack of bodily autonomy.

If I was treated this way, with all of the privilege I pos-sessed, with all eyes on Ferguson watching, *how do you think young Black people are treated when no members of the media are present to tell the story?* My mountains of privilege sur-rounded me with a cocoon of safety, and still I was beaten by police in the middle of the day with cameras watch-ing. But Black people fare much worse at the hands of the police. They are threatened. They are terrorized. They are beaten. They are imprisoned. They are disappeared—or worse.

Even more nerve-racking than the way that my body was responding to the arrest was my fears about the inevitable conflict that my arrest would stir up. I was physically sore from the arrest. I had panic attacks worrying about what people from my hometown would say, thinking about deal-ing with them on social media. It really says something about the stronghold white niceness had over me that I was more upset about Facebook notifications than being hit by a police baton.

I took a day off and then returned to protest with every-one else outside the Ferguson Police Department. I felt like I had to go back, to show that they hadn't scared us off, that we were full of even more resolve now. I didn't plan to stay too long this time, though, because I was helping facilitate a conversation with junior high students at an Episcopal church later that evening about the Uprising. Because I didn't plan on "marchin' alllll night long," and I had to show up as a professional later that evening, I arrived in work attire. Once again the other protesters teased me about showing up in heels and a navy pencil skirt that ended just above my bloodied knees.

That night after meeting with the high school youth group, my friend Rebecca Ragland and I headed to the police department in Ferguson again. We wanted to do some kind of reclaiming of that space after all that had happened there the weekend before. We packed up kneelers, and Rebecca brought her Communion kit. And in the parking lot of the Ferguson Police Department, we offered Communion to the protesters on an altar made of a protest sign that read, "Imagine Justice."

Psalm 23 is one of the most well-known and memorized parts of Scripture. It offers beautiful, pastoral imagery of green grass and still waters and a God who provides for our needs. But my favorite part of that Psalm is the section that comes a bit later:

> You [God] prepare a table before me
> in the presence of my enemies;
> you anoint my head with oil;
> my cup overflows.[5]

In the shadow of the deepest valley, enemies of justice expect freedom fighters to cower in fear. They think that with the threat of death all around us, they can make us bow down to their will on trembling knees. The powers and principalities think Black people and those who work for liberation should give up; they think we ought to be licking our wounds, or scared, or in hiding. But especially in the shadow of the valley of death, when it doesn't look like a time for celebration, God is there preparing a feast. God prepares before us a table in the presence of our enemies, a table so lavish and luxurious, a party so over the top that our cups are literally spilling over.

I sometimes joke that we should rename "Good Shepherd Sunday" to "God the Petty Party Planner Sunday" in reference to the second half of the Psalm. Because showing up in a shadowy place to throw a big ol' party in the face of our enemies is one of God's favorite things to do. God resists and protests all those death-dealing forces, and God does it in grand, delicious style. God takes our shadowy tombs and turns them into a bright Easter. God sets a table before us in the presence of our enemies, feeds us with God's own body, and tells us we never have to be afraid again.

That is something worth celebrating.

There were many moments of Communion, formally and informally, during the Uprising. Many of these communal meals were joyful. The activists made no apologies for this. When people or systems are plotting your death, every smile, every ounce of joy, every celebration, and every shout of hallelujah are resistance.

I learned this kind of joy-as-resistance from young Black organizers in Ferguson. Those protesters went right to the source, right to the seat of power, right to the Ferguson Police Department, to stare down those officers and chant Mike Brown's name, to let them know that we wouldn't forget what they had done to Lezley's son. And because for the first several months there were folks outside the police department 24/7, sometimes those folks had to eat.

Enter Cathy Daniels—better known as Mama Cat. Mama Cat held vigil with us, and she marched with us, although she moved slowly sometimes because she had a bad knee. But what Mama Cat most loved to do was feed us. "Food can heal you," she always said. "Everyone has an important role in the movement. It just so happens that mine is to care, to comfort, to nourish." And so she did. Every week outside the Ferguson PD, Mama Cat would bring over or cook food for hundreds of Ferguson protesters. And wow could Mama Cat cook. Sometimes she would bring simple snacks, but other times, it was an entire spread of barbecue or chicken—a full, proper cookout. The aroma of her cooking would waft through the air.

She would prepare a table for us across the police station, in the presence of the people who tear-gassed us, who shot rubber bullets at us, who tried to get us to cower, to run away in fear.

And so while many of our protests were serious and somber, at other times, they were filled with joy. There was dancing, food, parties. Sometimes we ordered pizza. A stubborn kind of community formed around these tables, a community of full bellies, a community of hope, a community of resistance that said to the powers and principalities of the police department, "You think you have the authority to steal all of these things from us, but there are some things you cannot take away."

Cocreating alongside God to bring forth a reign of justice and peace is hard work. But the reign of God is also full of joy. We are called to bring about this kingdom come "on earth as it is in Heaven." Communion is a moment built into our Christian liturgy where we get one of those glimpses. It is a moment out of time where we are joined with God and our ancestors and the saints of the past. We are gathered with our community in the present. And *we are casting a vision* for what is to come. In that vision, we are seated around a table where everyone has enough. Not only do people have their needs met; cups are running over. This is not a table of "just enough." This is not white bread and baloney. It is splendid and plentiful, full of essential nourishment and celebration. It's a full and proper cookout. It's a party that is catered by God where God gives us the very best They have to offer: God's own self.

In this vision for the future, everyone has a place and everyone is fed. Taste buds are dancing, cheeks are flushed, bellies are full. And that future is only possible if we pool our resources and redistribute them so that everyone has what they need. It is only possible if white Christians return stolen money, stolen labor, and stolen land. The systems and sins that rob our siblings may not have been constructed by us, but we inherited them, and we continue to benefit from them. They are our responsibility. It is capitalism and corporate greed that feeds racism and anti-Blackness in this country. Upending the entire system through a radical restructuring of wealth and resources is the only way we can build a world where Black lives matter. That is when we will be in right relationship with one another. That's when we get invited to the party, the feast, when this vision for the future becomes more than just a glimpse; it becomes reality.

Reflection Questions

1. What messages have you received about the importance of joy as a tool for social change (e.g., some people have been socialized to think of protesters dancing as frivolous as opposed to revolutionary)?
2. Has there been a time in your life where you did something joyful that felt like an act of rebellion against hate or evil?
3. Is there a time when you experienced joy during a period that was otherwise difficult?

4. Name a time in your life when eating food together with others built a sense of community. What was that like?
5. What do you experience in your body when you take Communion?
6. In what ways does Communion feel revolutionary to you?

Action Item

- Our current system includes disparities like food deserts, which make it harder for people in divested communities to gather around a shared meal where everyone's needs are met. Learn about food disparities in your community and how food justice is different from direct services like food pantries. Partner with organizations doing food justice work to lobby for a redistribution of resources to make sure that everyone has access to the table.

8

THE COST

I appeal to you therefore, [siblings], by the mercies of God, to
present your bodies as a living sacrifice, holy and acceptable to God,
which is your spiritual worship.

—Romans 12:1

I have noticed a strange phenomenon in white churches
in response to community organizing and activism. There
seems to be some sort of misconception that activism is
glamorous or cushy. I've seen this both with people who
are supportive of the movement and with detractors. Supporters seem to think activism is sexy work. They talk about
activists as if they are superheroes embroiled in an epic
battle. It is true that there are times I've felt a rush because
I could tell in my gut that I was part of something historic.
Even in a small way. Most of the time, though, activism is
full of less charming work.

Like meetings. So many meetings.

Detractors, on the other hand, seem to think that I enjoy being out in the streets, that it is fun for me to be in conflict. As I mentioned in the last chapter, activism can and should include moments of joy and celebration. But on the whole, no one I know thought that our time in the streets of Ferguson was "fun." We were normal people; we would much rather be reading romance novels, or playing video games, or sleeping, or doing almost anything else. Ferguson was powerful and meaningful. But it wasn't fun. The predominant emotional experience—for me, at least—was fear. And trauma.

Every July, you can find many Ferguson activists messaging each other in group texts from our basements. Hiding from fireworks that sound too much like tear-gas cannons. Once, when a firework went off near me unexpectedly in the middle of the day, I completely blacked out. I woke up to the sound of my own screaming as my spouse tried to comfort me and strangers stared.

I want to be very clear about this, because when we speak trivially about uprisings, we endanger people. This is not a game. There are real costs to this work, costs that I underestimated. I'm going to talk about some of the costs for me and my family because I want everyone to understand what activism is really like. But I want to reiterate: I was one of the most privileged people out there. I am a white woman. I had a job with a supportive boss. I had family and friends who believed in what I was doing. I had access to health care. And still, my body and mind will forever be different. As you read about the ways this work has affected me, keep in mind at every juncture how much more deeply Black activists are affected.

When I first started protesting, I didn't realize how much it would compound my former trauma. The lack of bodily autonomy afforded to me by police was difficult to bear as a sexual assault survivor. Watching white men abuse their authority would trigger me. I felt unsafe in my body so often in the streets. I thought that I knew that things would be hard, but I didn't realize how much old trauma would be uncovered for me. I had to learn that we bring our whole selves wherever we go. When I protest in the streets, I am my whole person. I carry my past within me. I don't get to leave certain parts of me on the shelf at home. I bring my identity as a survivor of sexual assault out in the streets with me, and there were many triggering moments. This is even more true, of course, for Black people, especially women and nonbinary people who are survivors of sexual violence.

I left Missouri in the fall of 2016 to attend seminary in Chicago. After a few years, I now recognize that I dissociated most of 2014 through 2016. There are large chunks of my memory missing, especially around traumatic events. Sometimes I am able to fill in the gaps with a video or photo. But other things I just don't remember. The things I do remember—and even my everyday life during that time—didn't feel like reality. It was as if I was reading a Choose Your Own Adventure book and could undo choices I made at any time. Nothing felt like it had consequences because nothing felt real.

This had huge repercussions for my marriage. I was undergoing a significant personal transformation faster than I ever had before. And I was very, very mentally unwell because of the things I was seeing and experiencing. I was on edge, constantly agitated. I felt like the only people who could understand me were other Ferguson protesters. And although Adam attended many actions during the Uprising, someone had to stay home with Alice during the nighttime protests, where police would be particularly violent. I was resentful that I was afraid and hurt and he wasn't there to protect me, even though I knew that thought was irrational. I would come home after days of terror, and he would come home after days of working in an office on calendars and PowerPoint presentations. He was in the military at the time (he now organizes with Veterans for Peace), but it felt like I was the one in the war zone. My eating disorder flared back up. I drank too much. I was acting out in my relationships and often lacking in boundaries. Once, during an argument, Adam unintentionally blocked the door, and I completely lost it. I felt trapped. It was too much like my abusive ex-boyfriend and too much like being kettled by the police.

Michael Brown was killed just a couple of months after our fourth wedding anniversary, but I honestly didn't know if our marriage would survive until our fifth. The only reason we made it is because Adam was incredibly compassionate and patient with me.

I was hypervigilant, on constant alert. But often for good reason. When I "cop-watched" or filmed the police during an encounter with a Black person, I was subject to harassment and intimidation. Police would try to tell me I didn't have the right to film them (I did) or that I was interfering with an arrest (I was nowhere near them). They would threaten to arrest me too. They would laugh at me. They would say they were going to confiscate my phone. A few times, after they released the person they were detaining, the police would follow me in my car for blocks.

The police tried at one point to use my activism to put Adam's career at risk. After I was arrested at the federal building in St. Louis in 2015, the police noticed that the address on my driver's license was from a military town outside of St. Louis. The police pretended to be friendly and chatted me up. I know better now. Now I would not speak to the police except to advocate for myself or a fellow arrestee to have things like medication, bathroom access, or medical attention.

But I was naive and thought that the surface-level pleasantries they were exchanging with me were harmless.

They used information from our conversation and found out that my spouse was in the military and that he was the one who would pick me up. Military members are discouraged from attending protests, and at that time, there was a travel advisory order against any military personnel going to St. Louis because of the Uprising. The next day, the police contacted Adam's superior officer, and he reprimanded Adam and told him to "get his wife under control." He had to meet with his superior officer and had documentation put in his file. He was lucky that the repercussions weren't greater.

Sometimes I felt paranoid. Other times I felt like I wasn't being vigilant enough. I received death threats daily on Twitter. Sometimes they would find my phone number. I received letters in the mail at my house, which scared me even more because that meant people knew where I lived, where my baby slept at night. The threats were frequently about my daughter. They would say horrible, racist things like "What monkey did you fuck to get that n***** daughter?" They would threaten to kidnap her or rape me.

I knew I couldn't call the police for help, not only because I don't believe in calling the police, but also because I was pretty convinced that some of the threats came from cops themselves. The threats sounded very similar to the racist language that the DOJ had uncovered in emails in multiple police departments. (It's worth noting, also, that in departments like Ferguson where tons of racist emails were discovered, there was not one email from even one police officer reporting the racist emails or pushing back against them in any way.) At the very least, these threats were from cop apologists. I knew the police wouldn't help us because they would think we deserved it. So I was new as an abolitionist, struggling to figure out safety without the cops. I had many meetings with my family and extended family about what to do in different scenarios. I role-played with my seven-year-old. I met with her school about their security policies, making them promise over and over they would never release her to someone who wasn't me or Adam.

Sometimes the reality of what was happening in Ferguson—and what has happened to Black and Brown and Indigenous people since the inception of policing—would just hit me, and I would fall apart. After the trauma of the night of the grand jury announcement and the militarized police response to our protests the next day, I left Missouri to visit my family in Iowa for Thanksgiving. When I was packing for the trip, I had this moment where I was transferring over the content of my purse to another purse. *OK, keys. Sunglasses. Wallet. Tear-gas kit.* I felt like I was going to throw up. It had gotten so normal to keep this tear-gas kit with me like a security blanket wherever I go. As normal as making sure I had my ID or car keys. The absurdity struck me at that moment; we are carrying around these things to defend ourselves from the people who had promised to protect us. I had choked on enough chemical weapons to begin to know for myself what Black people had known for centuries: the promise of protection was a lie. When I moved in 2016 to attend seminary, I continued to protest and get involved and connected with activism in Chicago. But it took a long time before I didn't carry my tear-gas kit with me everywhere.

And the Uprising wasn't just hard on my mental health and my relationships. My body was deeply affected too. I say often that my body has never been the same since Ferguson, and it is true. I am not the only one either. My hormones were disrupted by tear gas, and my periods were irregular despite being on birth control. My lung capacity decreased, and asthma that had not flared up since high school returned worse than ever. I began to have horrible, debilitating chronic pain that I live with to this day. I was eventually diagnosed with fibromyalgia, an illness that according to the Mayo Clinic can "be triggered by physical trauma" or "psychological stress."[1] And holy hell, was I psychologically stressed. I was constantly torn between worrying about the world my Black child was growing up in—wondering what would happen to her, desperate to keep her safe—and worrying about my own physical safety and even more about the safety of the Black activists in the streets with me.

The cost for me was real. It continues to affect me.

But I need you to know that there are people from the Uprising that lost so much more than I did.

In August 2015, I was part of a mass demonstration at the federal building in St. Louis urging the DOJ to do its job and hold the Ferguson Police Department accountable. We came to deliver a letter to a public official in the build-ing during normal business hours, and we were met with doors chained shut, barricades, and swarms of police. When we charged over the barricades and occupied the area in front of the locked building, cops began to arrest people. I watched as police officers walked around me to arrest Black people. I was right in front of them, but they sidestepped me to cuff a Black clergywoman or a Black teenager. This is why oftentimes when police begin to escalate, white allies are strategically brought to the front lines to prevent violence and arrests.

I easily avoided arrests. This is not true of the young Black leaders in the streets who were subject to random snatch-and-grab arrests without cause or provocation. Even when I was part of a planned action where I was participating in civil disobedience and intending to be arrested, the police would avoid arresting me because I was a short, young, white woman. Likewise, in addition to being one of the last people arrested at these actions, I was almost always the first or one of the first people released from jail after mass arrests. This has happened every time I have been arrested.

Those of us who had been arrested and then released quickly like to remind people of this:

Even with very brief stints in jail for protesting, *I have still spent more time in jail than Darren Wilson*—the cop who murdered Michael Brown.

Police target Black activists in a way I will never be targeted. Do not let anyone tell you that the Counter Intelligence Program (COINTELPRO) is a thing of the past. There is a concerted effort to target and disband Black liberation movements. It was not unusual during meetings or events for police to walk up and down the streets and run license plates for old warrants. These warrants were often for things like unpaid parking violations and other charges that function as poverty taxes. When people are locked up, even because of unpaid parking tickets and subsequent bench violations, they are at risk of losing their jobs, their homes, their children. The purpose of running plates was to have an excuse to arrest and intimidate people so that they won't protest because they fear retaliation.

When I was arrested during that mass action in 2015 with dozens of other protesters, we were charged with what amounted to blocking the doors of a building. It was a citation, not even a misdemeanor. It wasn't the type of violation that you normally arrest someone for. Usually, you just ticket them, at most. But once we were arrested, they took DNA swabs from all of us to have the DNA of dozens of activists on file. To me, this was a clear attempt at bolstering surveillance efforts to target Black activists and disrupt the movement. When we protested and asked why DNA swabs were even necessary, we were threatened with extended jail time.

People who are thought of as leaders in liberation movements are especially vulnerable to being targeted. This is one reason, in many cases, the current Movement for Black Lives resists central leadership figures. History has taught us, from MLK to Fred Hampton, that those people get assassinated. It is not unusual for police to intimidate Black activists they perceive as having influence and to arrest them on trumped-up charges.

Brittany Ferrell, for example, was charged with a felony when a car attempted to drive over a group of protesters occupying the freeway. The prosecutor alleged *she caused damage to the car that tried to mow her down*. The prosecutor that charged Brittany was Bob McCulloch, the same prosecutor who failed to indict Darren Wilson for the murder of Mike Brown and had been the target of many protests.

Police and prosecutors frequently overcharge Black people, and that is even truer when they are activists protesting the police. We like to pretend we don't have political prisoners in the United States, but many political prisoners are still locked up. Josh Williams, a.k.a. Kid Ferguson, is a famous example. He had just turned nineteen years old with no prior record when he was given *eight years* for allegedly lighting a trash can on fire—which caused no significant property damage. During his court proceedings, the prosecutor put the entire protest movement on trial. They talked about his involvement with the Uprising as evidence against his character. They did this in an attempt to make an example of Josh and intimidate others.

Black people have been fired from their jobs for protesting in this movement. They have lost their homes. They have lost their freedom. Some have lost their lives.

I met people in Ferguson who aren't here anymore. Several of their deaths are suspicious. Darren Seals was found shot to death in a burned-down car. His murder remains unsolved. Melissa McKinnies's son, Danye Jones, was found hanging from a tree. McKinnies was a protester in Ferguson and says that her family received death threats. The police ruled it a suicide. And there are more.

There are a lot of theories about who might be behind these suspicious deaths. But solving the deaths of protesters doesn't seem to be a top priority for the police.

There are other deaths too that we might not tie directly to protests at first glance. There are people who died of suicide, people who died of overdoses, people who died of heart issues or other stress-related illnesses. These are people who experienced months or years of police terror and harassment. Those experiences wear on a person's physical and mental health. Even in the cases of suicide or death by drugs due to self-medicating, I hold the police responsible for the psychological trauma they inflicted on people. White supremacy kills some people quickly, with a bullet in the streets. But it kills others slowly through dehumaniza-tion, deprivation of resources, and mental-emotional abuse.

These people—and all the victims of state violence—didn't have to die. And they will never be brought back. These are unspeakable losses.

I was protected by mountains of privilege, and my losses do not compare with what my Black counterparts experi-enced. I think it is important to be clear about that. I wanted to tell you about what I had experienced not so that you would feel sorry for me but because if this was the sort of stress I was under, you can only imagine what it was like for the young Black activists who were the true targets of police terror.

It is also important to be clear that antiracism work neces-sitates sacrifice. It is inherently risky because it involves challenging and disrupting the status quo. I sometimes wonder if part of the reason white people are so unprepared for racial justice work is that we are surprised by the cost.

There is a cost. It is real.

There are parts of my life and my health that I will never get back. As Christians, we are told by Jesus that if we are to follow him—a Brown man beaten by police and executed by the state—we will be marching toward our own crosses too. Jesus told his disciples in Matthew 16:24–25, "If any want to become my followers, let them deny themselves and take up their cross and follow me. For those who want to save their life will lose it, and those who lose their life for my sake will find it."

And yet the cost of abdicating my responsibility in this work is so much higher. Continuing in verse 26, Jesus says, "For what will it profit them if they gain the whole world but forfeit their life? Or what will they give in return for their life?"

The times I have failed to live into my ideals of antiracism, I have hurt people that I love. I have caused harm to my relationships and damage to my own soul. In those cases, I may have gained a whole world of privilege. But I have forfeited the life-giving connections that are so dear to me.

The losses I experienced because of the Uprising in Ferguson are real. But some of the things I lost were worth losing. I lost a great deal of naivete about the way that white supremacy functions in the world. I lost my belief in narratives around state violence and policing that are built entirely on lies. I lost my identity as a white moderate and traded it in for the identity of an abolitionist. I lost respectability in the eyes of a lot of white Christians who now found me to be too abrasive, too direct, too honest for their sensibilities.

I gained a lot too. I gained a better analysis of history and historical figures. I became more equipped to parent my Black children. I gained a greater understanding of the gospel of Jesus Christ.

And I gained relationships unlike any I've had before. My relationships from Ferguson help me comprehend God's dreams for the church in a new way. The Ferguson Fam is made up of all kinds of people. Many of us don't even always like each other. But we went through something together. We put our bodies on the line together for the sake of our collective liberation. We are bonded together, forever, because of the things we saw and did, side by side.

This baptism by tear gas changed how I think of community. Like in Christian baptism, I found a chosen family. In baptism we are brought into God's family under our Holy Parent. We are siblings, cousins, relatives, attached not by genetics but through the enduring mystical waters of Christ's death and resurrection.

These relationships matter. And they change us.

Washed in water or in tear gas, we are different.

Transformed.

You may not have been in Ferguson, but like we say— Ferguson is everywhere. Justice work looks different in different places, but in every context, people are working to build something new. You can be a part of a family, a coalition of people who are *in it* together. You can be transformed.

In any change, there is loss. You will have to sacrifice things like control, comfort, power, privilege, money, and resources. If you are a white person and you are not experiencing some discomfort or loss in antiracist work, you are not doing it right. This movement is not something you can visit as a tourist or observe and consume as a voyeur. It is a commitment. But the exchange will be more than worth it. Over time, you will build trust and deepen relationships. You will gain insight into yourself, your community, and the heart of God.

The lives and freedom of our Black, Brown, and Indigenous siblings are priceless. They are more than worth *any* cost. God knows this. And one day when our glimpses of liberation become our reality, history will know that too. Our descendants and future generations will ask us, "Where were you?" We will have to answer and be held accountable.

This is the gospel. The work is costly. And worth it.

Reflection Questions

1. Did you learn about COINTELPRO in school? If not, why do you think that is?
2. Elle talks about the ways that the cross has been hyperspiritualized. When you read the verse "take up [the]

cross and follow me,"[2] what do you think that "cross" refers to?

3. What sacrifices do you feel God is calling you to make to be in solidarity with your neighbor?

4. What price are you willing to pay for the sake of Black liberation?

5. What are you willing to leave behind in search of justice?

Action Items

- Donate to bail funds or funeral funds for victims of police violence. Learn about political prisoners—especially people of color—in your city or state. Provide them with material support.

- Get trained as a legal observer and then participate in protests to protect people's right to assembly.

- Learn about the history of COINTELPRO during the civil rights movement and the Black Power era.

- If you are a white person, follow the direction of Black and Brown and Indigenous leaders at protests, and if called upon, be ready to go to the front as a human shield.

9

TRANSFORMATION

Do not be conformed to this world, but be transformed by the
renewing of your minds, so that you may discern what is the will of
God—what is good and acceptable and perfect.

—Romans 12:2

In community organizing, we say that power is the ability to make change or influence things and that our power
resides in relationships. Relationships are the building
blocks of transformation. Building relationships is how
we build power. This includes getting clear with ourselves
about what is at stake for us in dismantling white supremacy, sharing our stories and our dreams, and hearing the
stories and dreams of others. The places where our dreams
overlap are where we start to get to work. That is how we
find our slice of it all.

Sometimes people ask how to get involved with the movement or how to find movement spaces. This is important. It is important, if you are able, to go into the streets to learn from the activists who are there. But it is just as important to take the sphere of influence and relationships you already have and *make them movement spaces*. This means your family, your workplace, your friend group, your church. Bring the voices from the streets and the lessons you learn there into those places.[1]

There are many roles in movement work. There are healers, storytellers, visionaries, artists, caregivers, and more. The church is made up of all kinds of individual people with all kinds of gifts. As individuals, they might be nurses or journalists or bookkeepers or mechanics or teachers or parents. Each of these skill sets has something to contribute, and your church is likely full of a diverse group of them.

The church as a whole, though, has a particular role to play.

We are inheritors of the sacred stories of our spiritual ancestors. Our ancestors saw glimpses of liberation too, and they dreamed together of what it might be like when those glimpses became reality. We are the keepers of these stories. We read them each Sunday. We teach them to our children. We make songs about them and sing them. We tell each other these stories over and over again because the pull of sinful systems is strong, and we need to be reminded.

Our ancestors dreamed of a world where prisoners are released and captives are set free, where debt is forgiven and wealth redistributed, where the yoke of slavery is torn off, where chains are broken.

This is consistent. These stories are throughout Scripture.

We have often told these stories as if they are metaphors, we have often repeated these promises as if we don't actually believe in them, and we have often forgotten that these stories are for us, here and now, too. The tendency of the church to depoliticize and decontextualize Scripture has ripped away its original intent as freedom literature. God wants people to be free from spiritual prisons, yes. But God also broke people, like the Apostle Peter, out of actual prison.[2] As preachers, parents, and Christian educators, we must stop divorcing the gospel from its material reality because Jesus cared very deeply about people's material reality. It was central to his ministry.

Jesus himself told us at the beginning of his ministry what the gospel is all about when he quoted the Prophet Isaiah and said,

> The spirit of the Lord God is upon me,
>   because the Lord has anointed me;
> [God] has sent me to bring good news to the oppressed,
>   to bind up the brokenhearted,
> to proclaim liberty to the captives,
>   and release to the prisoners.[3]

Jesus read this Scripture, this freedom dream of his ancestors, out loud and then said, "This is what I am all about."

The people who were there took him seriously. The Gospel of Luke tells us that the idea was provocative enough for them to try to hurl him off a cliff.

When I tell people I am a police and prison abolitionist, they are often skeptical at first. I was. But when I ask, "Do you think in heaven there are people in cages?" the answer is a clear and resounding no. We know that in God's reign, in the world that is coming, people are not imprisoned. We say we believe that God's will triumphs, that God's reign is unstoppable. And yet we resist the idea of a world without prisons and policing. If we truly believe what we say we believe, every Christian would be an abolitionist. We would know that the end of prisons and policing and the redistribution of resources to ensure that all are cared for are inevitable because those things are the will of God and we would rejoice that God is allowing us a role in making that world a reality sooner rather than later.

That is one of the special roles of the church: spiritual imagination.

We are people who believe in things not yet seen.

The church has not always been good stewards of this gift of spiritual imagination. In fact, there is evidence that modern penitentiaries are a Christian invention. So we have a responsibility as Christians to dismantle prisons.[4]

I became an abolitionist before I knew anything about all of the various alternative models of community safety and restorative justice that have been developed over the past sixty years or so to take the place of prisons and policing. What I did know was that our current system was wrong. It was immoral. It didn't deliver on promises to keep us safe. It divided us. It protected the interests of the few and sacrificed the many, extracting money and labor from Black and Brown people and the poor to feed the hungry beast of racialized capitalism.

I wasn't sure what was next. The abolitionists advocating for the end of slavery weren't either.

What I did have were glimpses. They were present in the sacred stories of Scripture. And they were present, tangibly, in the sacraments. In Communion, I have a vision of people who are gathered around a table. At this heavenly banquet table, as Pastor Lenny Duncan often says, Mike Brown is seated in the place of honor right next to Jesus. In the waters of baptism, I feel the cool splash of water initiating me into a radical family of God's beloved children. In the sound of the trickle of the font, I am reminded of the promise that through death and rebirth, impossible things can happen. Things can be better. Things can be transformed.

I've seen glimpses in the movement too.

The kingdom of God is like

Adam and Alice marching outside the jail, chanting, demanding my release and the release of other protesters, and staying there until we are all free.

The kingdom of God is like

a white bisexual woman with internalized biphobia who entered into a protest movement led in large part by queer Black women, who learned how to love herself and embrace her identity because she was first embraced by her LGBTQIA+ community.

The kingdom of God is like

a seven-year-old's eyes wide at night as she hears all creation cry out and whispers to her mom, "Even the wind is saying, 'Justice for Mike Brown.'"

The kingdom of God is like

being led away in handcuffs by a Black police officer. And when the arrestees start singing freedom songs, you hear him humming along under his breath too.

Some people ask me what will happen to police officers in this new world. I know that the reality for Black police officers is complicated. Many of them join the force because they want to change things. As a leader inside of an often unjust institution, the church, I understand it. The difference is that although the church has strayed from its mission and orchestrated endless atrocities, its original mission was one of love and liberation. Policing, on the other hand, was built on white supremacy, violence, and repression from the start. The script of white supremacy is so ingrained in policing that even if you substitute out the individual actors, regardless of race, the same story continues to play out. One of the police officers who killed George Floyd was Black.[5] He joined the force to change it. But the reality is, when you join a corrupt and dehumanizing institution, you don't change it. *It changes you.*

As a white person, it isn't appropriate for me to decide what is next for Black police officers. That is something for the Black community to decide.

But I will speak to white cops, many of whom are beginning to question the role that they have played. One white former police officer wrote about his belief in the necessity of abolition in a blog. Addressing his fellow officers, he asked, "Is this really the world you want to live in? Aren't you tired of the trauma? Aren't you tired of the soul sickness inherent to the badge? Aren't you tired of looking the other way when your partners break the law? Are you *really* willing to kill the next George Floyd, the next Breonna Taylor, the next Tamir Rice? How confident are you that your next use of force will be something you're proud of?"[6]

The police are welcome to repentance and accountability and to repair the harm they caused, like everyone else. Many of us are here, ready and waiting to receive them. I reject the imagery that I have heard some pastors use where Officer Darren Wilson is at the table seated next to Mike Brown. The reign of God does not put victims next to their abusers. It does not rely on coercive, weaponized forgiveness. When we hear stories of the lion lying down with the lamb in Scripture, what that means is that the lion has to change its ways. It has to alter its identity, its very nature, to stop being a predator. Otherwise, without that transformation, we are just continually offering up sheep to the slaughter.

I say sometimes that there are no cops in heaven.

It's a strong statement, but it's true. There aren't.

There are no cops in heaven because there are no cages in heaven. There are no police in heaven because there is no policing. When people who are cops have the opportunity to enter into the coming reign of God, they are welcome. But not as cops. They have to leave their guns and their badges and their participation in murderous, racist systems behind. Because there will be no place for those things in God's kin-dom.

Mother Mary's famous protest song in Luke 1 tells us that those who have been exalted, like police officers who are lionized in our current police state, will be made low. And those who have been treated as if they are lowly, like Michael Brown, will be brought up high. Darren Wilson might be present at the heavenly banquet, I don't know. But I imagine that if he is, he will spend at least some time *serving* Mike Brown, refilling his glass, bringing him his food.

This, too, is liberation. It is setting Darren free from his former role, transforming him by teaching him how to lie down with lambs without slaughtering them.

We can be transformed, not only individually but collectively. A Harvard political scientist, Erica Chenoweth, found that it takes 3.5 percent of the population participating actively in protests to create substantial, systemic change. In fact, if we look at history, once 3.5 percent of the population engages consistently in demonstrations, change is not only likely; it is *inevitable*.[7] In the United States, Christians make up 65 percent of the adult population.[8]

If the church acted powerfully, we could usher in the revolution.

While white supremacy is old, it was not baked into the foundations of the earth. There was a time before racism. There was a time before prisons and policing. There will be a time after. God's reign is coming. We can be a part of it, or we can oppose it. We can choose life or continue to worship the death cult of white supremacy. We can sacrifice our siblings, or we can forge bonds of solidarity with them. But this world is coming. It is closer every day.

Antiracism work is kingdom-building work. And Jesus made the coming kingdom possible, building the kingdom out of his own body.

Now the church is the body of Christ in the world.

> And God has sent you, us, the whole church
> to bring good news to the oppressed,
>   to bind up the brokenhearted,
> to proclaim liberty to the captives,
>   and release to the prisoners.

Amen.

Reflection Questions

1. How might your community help you discern the various roles you might play in the antiracist movement?

In what ways have you acted as a visionary, a teacher, a healer, an artist, or any other combination of roles?

2. Evaluate your spheres of influence. How might you contribute to them becoming more antiracist?

3. Elle refers to Scripture as the freedom stories of our ancestors. What Bible stories capture your spiritual imagination about the coming reign of God?

4. Elle says there are no cops in heaven because policing will be obsolete. What other oppressive institutions will no longer exist in heaven? Payday loan companies? Banks? What sorts of things will be present in their place?

5. Elle references the Harvard study that says it takes 3.5 percent of the population to participate in a protest on the streets to enact substantial change. What is holding the church back from being that 3.5 percent?

Action Items

- Familiarize yourself with the policy platform and action items for the Movement for Black Lives, a national coalition of Black liberation organizations including but not limited to Black Lives Matter at https://m4bl.org/.

- Discern within yourself and in relationship with others what your stake is in this work. Share your stories. Find where your dreams overlap. Choose your slice of this work and take action.

ACKNOWLEDGMENTS

So many people deserve my appreciation—more than I can remember, more than I could name. You have made me who I am. You made this book possible. I carry each of you with me in my heart. So knowing that my words will be inadequate in the face of my gratitude for all that I have been given, I want to say,

Thank you.

To the Triune God for your abundant grace. For showing us how to be in solidarity with one another. For your endless work in creating and liberating and loving us all.

To Alice and Jessica for showing me how to be brave. For doing a lot of dishes when I was too busy writing. For being the sweetest babies in the world. You are the reason I do everything that I do. My greatest hope is to build a world worthy of you. My biggest joy is being your mom.

To Adam for listening to me read this book in its entirety twice . . . after listening to me read it to you chapter by chapter. For calling me your "favorite theologian." For being my partner and confidante. For picking up the slack around the house. For being so faithfully devoted to me and the girls. For always supporting my goals and ideas, no matter the sacrifice, no matter how wild they may seem. For making it easier for me to be myself. You are better than a dream come true.

To Lisa Kloskin, my editor, who received my story so gently and held my hand throughout all of my anxiety in this process. To Jess Davis, my sensitivity editor, whose work on this book made me clearer in my message and who helped ensure that this project lives up to its ideals as much as possible. To Pastor Traci Blackmon for writing the foreword, for your transformational public witness and powerful preaching, and most importantly, for loving Alice and giving her such a faithful woman to look up to.

To Dr. Linda Thomas, my MDiv advisor and professor, and to Dr. JoAnne Marie Terrell for your wisdom, care, and guidance and for acquainting me more deeply with the theological brilliance of people like Dr. James Cone and others who have deeply informed my work.

To Dr. Benjamin Stewart for equipping me to talk sacramentally about the world around me and for brainstorming with me regarding other Lutheran theological connections for this book.

To Dr. Hector Avalos, who taught me to read the Bible critically and with an eye for power analysis.

To Gordy, of blessed memory, whose theology informs me every day, who taught me how to see the nonhuman world as full of relatives instead of resources to exploit, and who believed in me in the moments when the church doubted.

To my middle school teacher, Kate Safris, for acknowledging my passion for writing from a young age. To my high school teacher, Sarah Zdenek, for calling me a lioness before I had found my roar and for introducing me to Toni Morrison, Alice Walker, and many other authors that opened up new worlds for me. And to all of the other teachers and professors I have been fortunate enough to learn from throughout my life.

To Pastor Lenny Duncan for his counsel, advice, and dynamic example as a witness, a chronicler, and a pastor.

To Blue, my therapist, whose tenderness in processing a lot of these experiences empowered me to write about them.

To Tanya Watkins, Ab Weeks, and all of the activists and organizers with SOUL in Chicago. I feel so fortunate to be part of the struggle alongside you. Thank you for finding me a home in Chicago.

To Ali Ferin for literally everything. For being my friend, for listening to my ramblings and theological musing, for always being on my side, for giving me a godchild and turning me into an auntie of the cutest little ones, and, specifically, for helping write the discussion questions at the end of each chapter.

To my pastors, Pastor Lili and Pastor Liz, who nurtured my call and showed me that women like me could be leaders in ministry.

To the class of the Lutheran School of Theology at Chicago 2020, who endured so much together and who listened to me first make some of these theological connections in class. To Morgan for all the quality Sissy time and Maija for low-key joining our family and looking great in wedding pics with the girls. For the Triples: Sarah, Maddie, Corey, Ian. You are rad as hell, and I am honored to be your colleague in Christ's Church. For my other LSTC classmates and colleagues, especially Christina, River, Anne, Reed, Samantha, and Andrew, for your insight and friendship. For the Faith and Justice Collective and Thesis 96. The ministry you do is important and has meant a great deal to me.

To the babies I love so much, especially Gabe and Elias, Cece, and Ricky. You give me hope in God's promises and a fervor to fight for a better world.

To St. Luke's Lutheran Church in Logan Square. Our time together was instrumental in the creation of this book. It was written because of the themes I saw arising out of a year of preaching with you. Thank you, especially to the staff, Pastor Erin, Claire, Bev, and Carmen, and to the members of my committee, Brian, Sarena, Eric, and Debra.

To my friends, especially Chelsea, Katie, Kayla, Kathleen, Steph, Jessie, Lynnea, and Emily, for always cheering me on and encouraging me.

To our family and loved ones in Sierra Leone. To JCC for teaching me some Mende and how to cook cassava leaf. For your love and friendship and all that you have given me.

To my beloved siblings, Bubba, Dia, Enrique, and Madde, for your comfort and solidarity. For loving my babies and being someone that they can always turn to. For always hanging in there with me when things have been hard. For being my biggest fans and supporters. For letting me crash at your houses all the time when I need to get out of the city.

To my mom, the teeniest, tiniest Small Granny, for always speaking into existence the best things for me. For telling me I was a "make-it-happen kinda kid." For coming to Sierra Leone with me. For coming to Ferguson with me. For being radical right alongside me. For your help raising the girls. For everything.

To the Episcopal clergy of St. Louis, especially Bishop Smith, Rebecca, Amy, Mike, Teresa, Pamela, and Jon. For the youth of DioMo, especially the Diocesan Youth Advisory Council. For the interns at Deaconess Anne House, especially Peter, Martin, Bren, Jillian, Rosemary, Sherry, and Tori.

To the residents of Ferguson and St. Louis. To the activists and freedom fighters I met there. To Cathy for feeding my daughter pie at Cathy's Kitchen after my arrest so that she wouldn't be afraid. To Mama Cat, Pastor Starsky, Rabbi Susan, Rabbi Randy, KB, Phiwa, Cori, Maria,

Alicia, Tony, Lisha, Melissa, Diamond, Erika, Marcellus, Michelle, Cookie, Brittany, Netta, Alexis, Kayla, Brianna, Spann, Jermell, Josh, Angel, DeRay, the Costellos, the Lauras, Molly, Brenna, Justine, Emily, Bella, Rachel, Patricia, and so many more. To everyone who ate brunch with us at Mok's. To everyone whose work goes unnoticed. To everyone I forgot to mention. You are my heroes. You changed the world.

Most importantly, to Michael Brown's parents, family, and loved ones. We will make sure that his prophecy remains true—that the world will always know his name.

To Mike Brown.

Forever.

NOTES

Preface

1. "Making Abolition Geography in California's Central Valley with Ruth Wilson Gilmore," *Funambulist*, January–February 2019, https://tinyurl.com/yypx7jlv.
2. Angela Davis, "Angela Davis: This Moment Holds Possibilities for Change We Have Never before Experienced," June 10, 2020, YouTube video, https://www.youtube.com/watch?v=i3TU3QaarQE.
3. To give to Mike's mother's foundation, visit https://michaelodbrown.org/index.php/donate/. You can donate to Mike's father's foundation through PayPal (ChosenForChangeFund@gmail.com) or CashApp ($ChosenForChange).

Chapter 1

1. Wesley Lowery and Todd C. Frankel, "Mike Brown Notched a Hard-Fought Victory Just Days before He Was Shot: A Diploma," *Washington Post*, August 12, 2014, https://tinyurl.com/yya36luy.
2. Ionerlogan, "Michael Brown Was Only a Few Days Away from Being a College Student," *NewsOne*, August 15, 2014, https://tinyurl.com/y5akctuu.
3. At the time of writing this book, I have two Black daughters from Sierra Leone, Alice and Jessica. Alice came to the United States in 2013. Jessica did not come to the United States until 2017, so during the Ferguson Uprising, I only had one daughter living with me in the United States.
4. John 18:3, 12, 22.

5. James H. Cone, *The Cross and the Lynching Tree* (Maryknoll, NY: Orbis Books, 2013).

6. Joseph Bocko, *Luther's Small Catechism with African Descent Reflections* (Minneapolis, MN: Augsburg Fortress, 2019).

Chapter 2

1. "There Is No 5-Second Rule for the First Amendment, Ferguson," ACLU, August 21, 2014, https://tinyurl.com/y6tteh8y.

2. 1 Corinthians 12:7–12 NIV.

3. Rev. Martin Luther King Jr., "The Other America," speech at Grosse Pointe High School, March 14, 1968, https://www.crmvet.org/docs/otheram.htm.

4. You may notice that I said, "Say yes to an invitation." It is important that we do not insert ourselves into spaces not meant for us without invitation. If you are not in meaningful relationships where you are receiving invitations like this, do some reflection on why that might be.

5. Martin Luther, *Luther's Small Catechism with Explanation* (St. Louis: Concordia, 2017), 4.

Chapter 3

1. Robyn Roste, "8 Times John Lewis Inspired Us with His Faith and Optimism," Faith Strong Today, July 23, 2020, https://tinyurl.com/y2gdayeg.

2. Philippians 2.

3. Throughout this book, you might notice that I refer to God with various pronouns. Sometimes I use "She." Other times I use the nonbinary pronoun of "They." I sometimes use "He," but only when talking about Jesus specifically. This variety is intentional. We know that God is bigger than the societal boxes of gender. The different images we have of God serve to illuminate more about who God is. Each image has limitations. I try to use a variety of pronouns and images to round out our mental picture of God.

4. Exodus 20:2.

5. Trymaine Lee, "Ferguson Protesters Win Injunction to Stop Cops Using Tear Gas," *MSNBC*, December 11, 2014, https://tinyurl.com/l3post4.

6. Danny Wicentowski, "New Video of MoKaBe's Tear-Gassing Raises Questions about St. Louis Police Tactics," *Riverfront Times*, December 11, 2014, https://tinyurl.com/yxflzuc8.

7. Michel Martin, "Racism Is Literally Bad for Your Health," *NPR*, October 28, 2017, https://tinyurl.com/yccvx3ho.

8. Martin Luther King Jr., "Letter from a Birmingham Jail," Estate of Martin Luther King Jr., April 16, 1963, https://tinyurl.com/o5te8je.

9. Blythe Bernhard, "Life Expectancy in St. Louis Depends Greatly on Geography," *St. Louis Post-Dispatch*, August 3, 2016, https://tinyurl.com/yyee77n6.

10. Jeremiah 6:14.

11. J. M. Casas, "Ferguson Protest Art Finds a Final Resting Place," St. Louis Public Radio, September 27, 2016, https://tinyurl.com/yxrcxu9r.

12. "About Us," Mirror Casket Project, accessed May 30, 2020, https://mirrorcasket.com/aboutus.

Chapter 4

1. Isabella Rosario, "Jesus Was Divisive: A Black Pastor's Message to White Christians," *NPR*, June 12, 2020, https://tinyurl.com/y9yooray.

2. "Feds Opposed Releasing Ferguson Robbery Video," *CBS News*, August 16, 2014, https://tinyurl.com/y5m3gyk5.

3. Ida B. Wells, "Southern Horrors: Lynch Law in All Its Phases" (Tremont Temple, Boston Monday Lectureship, February 13, 1893); see also https://tinyurl.com/yxteumds.

4. This last line is a reference to Marx. Assata Shakur and other visionary Black freedom fighters see capitalism as intricately intertwined with anti-Black oppression.

5. Richard Pérez-Peña, "Woman Linked to 1955 Emmett Till Murder Tells Historians Her Claims Were False," *New York Times*, January 27, 2017, https://tinyurl.com/ja7we4y.

6. Amir Vera and Laura Ly, "White Woman Who Called Police on a Black Man Bird-Watching in Central Park Has Been Fired," *CNN*, May 26, 2020, https://tinyurl.com/yb739e9b.

7.   Beverly Daniel Tatum, *Why Are All the Black Kids Sitting Together in the Cafeteria? And Other Conversations about Race* (New York: Basic Books, 1997).

Chapter 5

1.   "Prosecutor in Michael Brown Case Has Deep Family Ties to Police," *NBC News*, August 20, 2014, https://tinyurl.com/y243mzcb.

2.   Dara Lind, "Prosecutors Grossly Mishandled the Darren Wilson Investigation," *Vox*, November 26, 2014, https://tinyurl.com/yypyqcgn.

3.   Episcopal Church, *The Book of Common Prayer and Administration of the Sacraments and Other Rites and Ceremonies of the Church: Together with the Psalter or Psalms of David According to the Use of the Episcopal Church* (New York: Seabury Press, 1979), hymn 483.

4.   I experience so much privilege. And in the moments where that is especially in play, I notice this lack of endurance. As a bisexual person and a woman who has experienced other forms of oppression, I have also noticed my own tenacity in the face of oppression where my cisgender heterosexual siblings often tire out.

5.   Tertullian, *Apologeticum*, L3 (197); see also http://www.tertullian.org/works/apologeticum.htm.

6.   Ilana Sichel, "The Nazi History of This Yiddish Protest Banner," Jewniverse, January 23, 2017, https://tinyurl.com/y6kuf48l.

7.   Blue Telusma, "Is the 'Strong Black Woman' Stereotype Killing Us? A Study Says Yes, but There Are Alternatives," theGrio, May 28, 2019, https://tinyurl.com/y2wvveqw.

8.   Reminder: throughout this book, you might notice that I refer to God with various pronouns. Sometimes I use "She." Other times I use the nonbinary pronoun of "They." I sometimes use "He," but only when talking about Jesus specifically. This variety is intentional. We know that God is bigger than the societal boxes of gender. The different images we have of God serve to illuminate more about who God is. Each image has limitations. I try to use a variety of pronouns and images to round out our mental picture of God.

Chapter 6

1. Associated Press, "King's Widow Urges Acts of Compassion," *Los Angeles Times*, January 17, 2000, https://tinyurl.com/y3k2exmb.
2. Audre Lorde, "The Master's Tools Will Never Dismantle the Master's House," Catalyst Project: Anti-Racism for Collective Liberation, January 2013, https://tinyurl.com/yb3o62kh.
3. Erin N. Winkler, "Children Are Not Colorblind: How Young Children Learn Race," University of Wisconsin-Milwaukee, November 2017, https://tinyurl.com/y58nrz6h.
4. Danielle Buhuro, *Spiritual Care in the Age of #BlackLivesMatter* (Eugene, OR: Cascade Books, 2019).
5. Matthew 11:28.
6. Any time we support other people, it is important to listen to what they say their needs are. White people should take special care to avoid condescending or infantilizing people and should not assume what Black activists or any people of color need.

Chapter 7

1. Quoted from a panel event, "Why Protest?," Christ Church Cathedral, March 8, 2015.
2. Associated Press, "King's Widow Urges Acts of Compassion."
3. Justin Fenton, "Baltimore Police Officer Charged in BB Gun Planting Incident as Gun Trace Task Force Fallout Continues," *Baltimore Sun*, January 15, 2020, https://tinyurl.com/y39zr5rf.
4. Tim O'Neil, "St. Louis Police Officer Had Cocaine in System during Crash, Prosecutor Says," *St. Louis Post-Dispatch*, January 27, 2016, https://tinyurl.com/y3t6yjpl.
5. Psalm 23:5.

Chapter 8

1. Mayo Clinic Staff, "Fibromyalgia Symptoms and Causes," Mayo Clinic, October 7, 2020, https://tinyurl.com/y2wz4hr4.
2. Matthew 16:24.

Chapter 9

1. Those of us who are disabled may not be able to be present physically, but your contributions to this movement are still important. There are ways to "show up" for liberation despite the many
   barriers in accessibility present in participating in direct actions.
   These ways vary from place to place, and so disabled activists
   are the best people to ask how to plug in where you are. For those
   of us who are not disabled, it is important to work to remove
   barriers to accessibility in our liberation movements.
2. Acts 12.
3. Isaiah 61:1.
4. Christopher D. Marshall, "Prison, Prisoners, and the Bible" (paper
   presented at the Breaking Down the Walls Conference, June
   2002), 4, https://tinyurl.com/y3aqgc9s.
5. Kim Barker, "The Black Officer Who Detained George Floyd Had
   Pledge to Fix the Police," *New York Times*, June 27, 2020, https://
   tinyurl.com/y9kxd4yh.
6. Officer A. Cab, "Confessions of a Former Bastard Cop," *Medium*,
   June 6, 2020, https://tinyurl.com/y9pqr5gk.
7. David Robson, "'The 3.5% Rule': How a Small Minority Can
   Change the World," *BBC Future*, May 13, 2019, https://tinyurl
   .com/y2vra84j.
8. David Crary, "Share of Americans with No Religious Affiliation
   Growing," *U.S. News & World Report*, October 17, 2019, https://
   tinyurl.com/y6hgk8od.